Once Lost Now Found

A Memoir

by: Brielle

WESTBOW
PRESS°
A DIVISION OF THOMAS NELSON
& ZONDERVAN

WestBow Press books may be ordered through booksellers or by contacting:

WestBow Press
A Division of Thomas Nelson & Zondervan
1663 Liberty Drive
Bloomington, IN 47403
www.westbowpress.com
844-714-3454

Scripture marked (NKJV) taken from the New King James Version®. Copyright © 1982 by Thomas Nelson. Used by permission. All rights reserved.

ISBN: 979-8-3850-0591-8 (sc)
ISBN: 979-8-3850-0592-5 (hc)
ISBN: 979-8-3850-0593-2 (e)

Library of Congress Control Number: 2023916310

Print information available on the last page.

WestBow Press rev. date: 09/07/2023

This book is a love letter to those who have been lost, heartbroken, discarded, abused, and abandoned by men. This story is for those who never experienced a father's love. God sees you. I pray my memoir speaks to the brokenhearted. I'm here to tell you of the loving-kindnesses of the Lord who found me. And I write this in the hope you'll find Him through my story.

I dedicate this book to my best friend in heaven, Caroline. I miss you every day, Carrie. Thank you for encouraging me to write this book.

God, thank you. This is Yours.

Jesus answered and said to him, "If anyone loves Me, he will keep My word; and My Father will love him, and We will come to him and make Our home with him."
—*John 14:23*

Contents

Chapter One

CINDERELLA

Here I am, Brielle, in a sparkling aquamarine ball gown and a silver tiara. For the first time in my life, this tomboy is looking like Cinderella. It's time to step out in the light, in the center of the ballroom. I am the center of attention, oh my.

There's a whole crowd of people I love. The family from Barbados and New York, friends I haven't seen in forever, and people who have been by my side since first grade. They are all here to see me. It's my sweet-sixteen day. My eyes endlessly look around the room, and I am feeling open and exposed.

Suddenly, I look into the eyes of the man across the room, and my anxiousness and fearfulness instantly start to fade away. His eyes locked on mine bring me peace and hope. This one man caught my eye out of seventy people. I've never seen anyone look at me the way he is. His is a look of wonder, care, captured love, and unspoken dreams.

It is the type of gaze that makes time stop for me. There is nothing bad in the world while he keeps his eyes on me. It feels like he is looking at everything good, his greatest accomplishment, his one and only—the one he is most proud of. He is looking at his princess, his everything, his Cinderella.

He begins to approach me as the song "Cinderella" by Steven

Curtis Chapman starts. He reaches out his hand toward me, and my heart stops. My daddy! He takes my hand, and I hold him. He pulls me in, he holds me tight, he leads me, and he guides my feet to dance. As we take our first steps together, I begin to think of all the times I placed my feet on his in the kitchen of our home. Ever since I was a little girl, we were dancing in that kitchen, and since then I've never stopped dancing, always imagining I'm on my daddy's feet.

Every breath is heavy. This is my reality. I can't believe this special moment is my life. Someone pinch me—but please don't.

I begin to feel like the most special girl in the world. I am safe in Daddy's arms. Tears fall down my cheeks, his eyes hold mine, and I never want to leave because every second with him is all I need. Time slows, and I never want to let go. At this moment, I'm Cinderella, my shoe fits, and I'm right where I'm meant to be. I am in the arms of my daddy.

All I hoped for was to feel like Cinderella forever, that time could stand still, and that I could feel this love all the time. This love was so safe, without worry in the world. This was what my heart yearned for—to love and to be loved forever.

This is the story of a Daddy's girl, a girl who felt so loved, a joyful girl, a beautiful girl. Every girl wants to be a princess, especially to her father.

Growing up, I was my dad's best friend, and the biggest fan of everything he did, especially soccer. My dad was my coach, my protector, my hero. I've always been the girl who trusted her dad with all her heart, who saw him as her strong protector from everything bad in the world. I wanted to make him proud in every way possible.

I wanted him to stay home instead of going to work. When my hero walked through the door at the end of the day, I would massage his shoulders and back. I needed his warm embrace more than I thought. My dad took care of my broken bones and hurtful pains.

I used to be the girl who always called when I needed him, which seemed like every hour, and probably was. I was the daddy's girl who dreamed of having a husband like her dad someday. I wanted someone who laughed endlessly, whose smile lit up the room, who was full of humor and silliness, and I wanted someone I could tell everything to, even the hard stuff.

I was the girl who wanted to give back all I could because of all my father's hard work. I wanted him to rest instead of working so hard all the time because I cared about every aspect of his life. I was the teenager who saw his pain and wanted to help, who loved everything about him. I was the daddy's girl who practiced dancing with her feet on top of his feet and waited for every next dance with him. I yearned for that father-daughter dance in front of everyone again, just one more time.

I always saw the good in him. And I was privileged to experience his unconditional love. I understood that love must be like this or more of this. There is something extraordinary about being someone's Cinderella.

With my dad, I always wanted to know more, to be taught more. My dad taught me almost everything I know. He was my example of how to raise children, how to live, and how to love. He was the one who taught me to ride a bike and to never give up. He taught me that it was OK to win, and it was OK to be upset when I lose. He taught me that failing is not the end. He taught me how to withstand it when things get hard and not just crumble.

One of the greatest life lessons I learned from my dad is to never say goodbye. My dad never said goodbye to me. He always said, "See you later." I've kept that in my heart and have always let the words "See you later" come out of my mouth because of him. With my daddy, there will never be a goodbye. No one ever wants to say goodbye to their loved ones.

Little did I know that this lesson would be my breaking, a sad reality. My sweet sixteen was the last time I let my dad's eyes hold mine—my last perfect memory of being a daddy's girl, of being his Cinderella.

Chapter Two

CITY BOY AND FARM GIRL

Two years after my sweet sixteen, on June 9, 2017, my whole family went to visit my grandparents in Barbados, a beautiful island near Puerto Rico. Both my parents grew up there, my dad in a small town and my mom on a big farm.

My dad always said, "How do complete opposites find each other, a city boy and a farm girl, meeting on this beautiful island we call home, how could it be?"

I guess they were just meant to be. Their story is quite incredible. Let me tell you a little about them before I tell you about our family trip.

Once upon a time, there was a young city boy and a young farm girl who lived on this very small island. The young city boy grew up with four siblings—two brothers and two sisters. His dad worked constantly, and his mom took care of them.

This city boy grew up poor, playing soccer barefoot with trash cans as goals. Sometimes he would come home with bleeding feet from running around outside all day causing trouble in the streets. The stories he had were endless.

This city boy was filled with adventure, impulse, and no fear. This city boy started out timid but turned into a fighter—a fighter in every way. He grew up fighting for everything he had and never stopped. What was worth fighting for in his life?

One day during primary school, he spotted my mom, the farm girl with very long beautiful hair and very light skin. *Mulatto girl*, he called her, which meant Black and White race. He saw how radiant she was and wanted to get to know her, so he did. Maybe she would be someone he would fight for.

This farm girl was raised by her mother and grandpa because her dad left her and her siblings behind. She was the oldest child, a big sister to her younger brother and sister. She had an absentee alcoholic father who never stayed. I wonder if this farm girl ever thought she was worth fighting for. Her dad never fought for her.

For unknown reasons, this farm girl was very soft-spoken, super-quiet, a mystery girl, an incredible listener, and impressively talented in the arts. She could design anything with her hands. And the city boy could do everything with his hands.

Spiritually, these two both grew up attending church school. The city boy's mother kept him in the church choir, while the farm girl's mom kept her in prayer with God and following God. Her mom taught her the purpose of a relationship with God.

Sometimes these very different people would walk home from school together as they continued to get to know each other. They lived a simple life. They began to date in their teens. Soon they began to share their dreams with each other, dreams filled with wonder and hope for their futures. How would their relationship collide in this journey?

This city boy dreamed of going to an even bigger city, where all dreams were possible. New York City was a dream place where anyone could be anything they wanted to be. City boy would soon be moving to New York, to his aunt's apartment with his dad and older brother. City boy was sixteen when he wrote letters from the States to his sweetheart farm girl, but he was so busy hustling and bustling to make it that letters slowly stopped being sent across sea.

Somehow, they remained hopeful. The farm girl had dreams of being a designer, as she made her own clothes—even her future wedding dress. She thought maybe she could be a designer in the States with the city boy.

While the farm girl daydreamed, the city boy was chasing his dreams in the place he thought would naturally be a dream come true. He worked many hours to help his dad, and soon entered college. The farm girl, for her part, was soon coming to the States to be with her city boy, so they could marry and pick up where they left off. They were planning to marry even with so much time and distance between them.

The farm girl arrived in the US at about nineteen with her sister, leaving her mother, brother, and grandpa behind. She and the city boy were to be married while they were in their twenties. These starstruck lovers traveled across seas together and married on the small island they called home. A beautiful wedding—a wedding I hope to repeat someday.

The farm girl wore a dazzling long-sleeved, beaded, fitted dress—a stunning, captivating Cinderella. The bridesmaids wore all different colors to match the island: pink, blue, yellow, green, and purple. The groomsmen wore white suits with their boutonnieres matching the bridesmaids' dress colors, which again filled the beach with extravagant color.

The ceremony was on the beach. I'm sure all eyes were on the bride. These starstruck lovers finally tied the knot after distance, green cards, citizenship, lost letters, shattered dreams, and many moments of time tried to come between them. The farm girl and the city boy lived happily ever after. Or I assumed they did.

Chapter Three

LOST SLIPPER

The city boy and the farm girl lived happily ever after … for a few years, with the normal struggles of life. They accumulated some debt, bought a home, and had five kids—my four brothers and me. Their fairy tale was never really a fairy tale like Cinderella's, though. After about twenty years, the fantasy started to crack, as the city boy and farm girl grew and changed.

Their union separated slowly, and then unexpectedly quickly. It was June 19, 2017, on that beautiful island they once called home where their love story began to slip away, from fairy tale to nightmare. It was our family vacation—the vacation that changed it all. The calm before the storm.

On a beautiful summer morning, we all were packed to catch our flight at the airport. It was a normal day, yet I felt like something was brewing behind the scenes. My parents wanted to go back home, but there was also a sense of secrecy, silence, and sadness. I could feel it, but I had no idea what it was or where it came from.

I thought maybe it'd just been such a long time since they were back in their hometown, the place where their fairy tale started. A place of memories, good and bad, lovely and ugly. A place where I was once just thought about. A place we could all come back to someday. This would be my first time seeing my grandparents on my dad's side, in the new home they built.

As we entered the airport, my whole family rushed in. My cousin and my uncle were coming with us. My uncle and my dad are the closest brothers you could ever imagine. They used to cause chaos together, switch identities in school, race each other, teach each other, protect each other, and were always so loyal to each other. They've always shared genuine brotherly love.

In the airport, we all couldn't stop laughing at their nonsense. The whole airport could hear them while they were drinking beer together, with their strange accents and broken English dialect. When those two got together, there most likely would be a fight, many tears of laughter, hurt feelings, or all of the above. Those two are very hardcore guys, and if instigated, they can go from 0 to 100. They could be calm laughing one second and then explode with rage the next.

Finally, we began to board the plane. My dad and his brother were giggling from having a little Hennessy. As soon as we sat down, my dad passed out and slept throughout the whole flight. It was hilarious, because at that point, a plane crash wouldn't wake him up.

Vacation was the only time my dad got more than four or five hours of sleep. We kids all had a feeling that they planned this drinking thing out from the start so they would both be able to sleep the whole flight. Meanwhile, I hated flying and still do, just because I get bad motion sickness, nausea, and insane ear-popping. This feeling is unbearable for me sometimes. Thank God the flight wasn't too long—only four hours.

As we rented a truck to get to the mainland, I wondered if things felt this way because Dad was stressed with work, if he was worried about his dad's cancer, or maybe he was just angry at the world or miserable with his life. Suddenly, as we were driving, soon to arrive, memories came flooding of all the times Dad would have moments of anger, whether it was because of us kids, work, or just life.

I could never get out of my head the memory of the time he punched a hole in the wall. Dad always had a short fuse, and sometimes I was scared, but mostly I was sad because I couldn't understand what he was feeling, and I wanted to know. He never took the time to explain what was going on with him emotionally; he would only lash out with emotion and say things like *I'm tired of this nonsense* or *This isn't living. I should drop all of this and leave you kids here with Mom,* and other statements I don't want to remember.

His statements about leaving always hurt me the most. I used to have thoughts in my head like, *But you never say goodbye, you only say "see you later." What do you mean you should leave?* I was a daddy's girl confused by her dad. What happened? Was Cinderella not enough anymore to be his princess? Would he want to leave his Brielle?

We finally got to my grandparents' new house. Granddad looked strong even with cancer, Nana was cute as a button, and this house was a dream—my grandparents' dream come true. I glimpsed over at my dad, and I could see his wandering eyes filled with questions, filled with memories. I wished I could know what he was thinking.

All my brothers were getting ready to go out on an adventure by the cliff at the beach, and I was getting ready to hang out with my cousin for an adventure as well. I caught my mom's eyes, her timid eyes, also wondering. I could tell she wanted to see her mom, and she was reminiscing just like Dad. They were both home, yet they both seemed out of place, almost like they needed to experience home again.

Later on that first night, all I noticed was this feeling I couldn't understand. I felt everything that was wrong, stimulating senses I wanted to go away.

That same night, my mom had a dream—a dream about my dad, a dream she told me about. In the dream, Mom was with Dad at a bar. There were dark bar lights, and my dad went to the bathroom, so Mom stayed at the bar waiting for him to come back. Time passed, and she wondered where he was. She went looking for him in the bathroom—this bathroom with red doors, gloomy doors—and she saw her husband kissing this dark-haired girl in the bathroom.

When she told me, I couldn't bear it, I couldn't believe it, and I didn't want to hear it. Dad wouldn't do such a thing, and my mom believed that he wouldn't too.

The next morning, I pondered on it, but I didn't let it take over my trip. It was just a dream, and my dad would never. Yet I still couldn't shake that uncomfortable feeling between my parents the whole rest of the trip.

For years, my dad would have anger tantrums about leaving us kids with our mom. He would always say what he felt and thought, even if it hurt someone else. Because he was miserable, it seemed like he wanted everyone else to be miserable with him. I have no idea what he was going through internally, in his heart, but I always knew it was very deep-rooted stuff that he never came to terms with. You know the saying, "Hurt people hurt people."

We always knew something was wrong. He struggled, but he would never talk about it with us. He never revealed his heart's true feelings, his heart's true pain. I felt like all these things started to happen when he stopped coaching me and started to work even more, more overtime, and longer hours.

Not only was my dad struggling, but my mom was as well. She was always so isolated, never expressing her feelings. If you were lucky, maybe she would say something real with a lot of passion. With her, it was, and sometimes still is, like peeling back layer after layer to figure out who she truly is.

Growing up, it always seemed like they both needed to just scream and let everything out, but they never did because of fear. The Barbados trip was when the family devastation seemed to begin, but I knew it really began long ago after my dad stopped coaching me.

———

In the dream my mom had in Barbados, my dad cheated on her at a bar. She knew it vividly, but she didn't tell anyone for about a month. As the trip ended and we got home, my discomfort grew and grew. Something was seriously wrong, and I felt it all the time, and I just knew it was about my dad.

My mom decided to confess to me what she knew to be true. At the time, we were driving to church for the eight o'clock. service. I felt the heaviness in the car, but I already knew that my dad was cheating before my mom even opened her mouth.

For a while, I'd dismissed what I saw. My dad would leave for work early and come back home late or at random times in the day. He started closing his door a lot and secretly making calls. He would linger in his car for long periods of time and always make some random comment or excuse to leave.

I knew he was lying to me almost every time he left the house. In the meantime, my mom asked me a lot of questions about him almost every day, as I saw her get quieter and quieter, her light slowly dimming, her thoughts seeming more calculated by the minute.

In the car before church, my heart started beating like a stampede, so I said, "Mom, I already know Dad is cheating." I told her how I knew from the very start. She remained calm and began to tell me all she knew.

She'd found bank-statement transactions to lingerie stores, perfume stores, jewelry stores, and hotel bookings. He had a whole other card for his lover and her kid. He was giving her money every month to help her and her child. My mom assumed she worked with him.

As she confessed all of this at once, I couldn't believe what I was hearing. How could my intuition be correct? God knew I didn't want to be right about this. In my head, I thought, *This can't be my life. Mom doesn't deserve this.*

As I was trying to deny this and keep it from killing me, she told me how he would pack extra bags in his car. She would know this by peeking through her bedroom window every night.

Silence rushed over me. I took deep sighs, "What am I supposed to say? I'm so sorry, but what are you going to do?"

Mom said, "I'm not going to confront him yet. I don't have enough evidence so he can't deny it. I want to see if he confesses without the evidence."

We arrived at church. My head and eyes felt like a thousand pounds trying not to cry in front of her, hoping she didn't regret telling me. My mind and heart started to fill with disappointment, anger, and sadness as I walked into the church and into the pew where we always sit. Man, I could barely stand.

At that moment, I felt like dying would be easier. Breathing hurt. Thinking made no sense. Feeling seemed pointless. Love felt like murder. Everything I thought was good felt like a lie. I thought, *How can he be paying for this woman and her kid? Why does he complain about money and about not making enough, or stressing about us all becoming rich?*

He repeatedly would tell us kids that he put food on the table, as he would make statements about leaving us here with our mother. *Is that what he wants, to leave us? Does he hate us? Does he wish we didn't exist? Do men just lie to the ones they love one day or every day? How can I trust anything he says? I can't!*

My thoughts were racing. *Does he not care about us anymore? How could he feel this way? Does he not care about our hearts? Is this woman more important than his family? Did we do something wrong? I hate that you did this, Daddy, how could you do this? I thought you were a good man. My mom is so amazing, how could you? I thought you were my hero. I thought I could trust you, Daddy. I thought you were loyal. You can have your wish, Dad, you can leave! I thought you were our protector and no one else's. I thought wrong.*

This broken heart I had felt like heart cancer; it started off slow and built and built, devoured, and killed everything good in its path. My heart became infected, and I was in need of chemo. Maybe chemo would be the answer for healing. It was possible that it could fix this heartbreak, but would it? And yet, there was still a chance I might die of this sorrow.

My own heart was attacking itself with grief and loss—grief that maybe I could have lived a better life and chosen a different path. Was there any way of preventing this?

This heart cancer devoured me in the loss of all the things I used to believe. I used to be free of regret and shame, free of resentment and disappointment. I used to be a princess entangled in her good life with her good dad. This loss allowed no joy in. This cancer of the heart consumed me. It was dark and painful.

Daddy, you felt dead to me. The minute it was all true, I lost you. I lost hope in you. I lost trust in you. I lost your smile. I lost your laugh. I lost your strength. I lost your protection from all the evil in men I met. I lost your touch. I lost your voice of reason and passion. I lost my fight. I lost my truth. I lost my dance partner. I lost the one who would save me at midnight and who would carry me when my glass slipper was lost. I lost the way I would walk through life in confidence. I wanted to walk in your footsteps. Most of all, I lost my father. And while losing you, I lost me.

—∞—

After church that morning, days went by as my life changed. My heart cancer only grew, and Cinderella lost more than her slipper. Mom started to bring proof to Dad, not accusing, but bringing forth all the evidence. Day after day, he would deny it all with the proof right in front of him. He would say, "I just gave her some money because she was struggling to pay for her child." My mom would tell me no man would do this unless he was getting something in return. Dad was always a giving man, but we never thought it would lead to the wrong intentions.

He made many mistakes with this woman that would cost him his whole family. He'd never given money to a woman before unless she was homeless. Mom believed this woman worked with him, because she lived somewhere near my dad's work.

More days would pass, but Mom continued to look through the window with tears in her eyes. Every time he left her, she knew he was leaving to be with another woman. My mother's beautiful sweet eyes became empty. She had glassy eyes filled with only pain, empty of all life. The heart cancer somehow didn't kill me every time I saw my mom become this withered person, a small fragment of herself, a tired believer.

More days passed, but Dad continued to lie about everything. His eyes weren't filled with regret or shame. Those weren't my dad's eyes, so I stopped looking at him. I couldn't look at him. He'd died in my eyes.

A yell, a scream, a silence. A yell, a scream, a silence. We were all just kids hearing someone who sounded like Mom screaming. Mom never screamed or threw things. Her anger scared me, like how Dad's anger used to do. She'd had enough of the lies. And instantly I thought, *Will I lose her too?*

Sometimes I would listen to the fights, if I needed to be home. She would give him a choice to sleep downstairs or wherever he wanted. I grew to prefer screaming and things smashing to silence. Silence made things seem like none of it would change. The silence made the unending pain of it all loud in my soul. Silence seemed like an eternity, hopeless even.

I hated the silence because even I was silent. Nothing came out of me, not a word. I was like a mute, frozen, weak, paralyzed. *God, will this end?* The silence felt like meningitis, bacteria that elevated fluid in the brain slowly. Then out of nowhere, the bacteria encompassed me into this coma. Without antibiotics and draining out the cerebral spinal fluid slowly, I could stay in a coma or die.

I knew no doctor, no man, could get me out of this coma. *God, you're the only one who can get me out of this coma.* My thoughts, fears, and tears elevated slowly at first. Slowly and then quickly, the silence made me comatose, void, numb. I cried out for help, for a cure to this pain, an antidote that I knew wouldn't come. I needed the growing pains to cease, something to drain me of my racing thoughts, my troubled brain. *Will I ever be sane, will I ever not be in pain, can I survive this silent coma?*

I wondered about the fighting and the lying. Did Dad experience this coma too? Or was he the cancer or the bacteria?

Cinderella's dad died that day. I was never the same. How could I be? He left a mark and left my mom broken and alone. He left us in a house that was no longer a home. I suffered more hurt from the people around me, the people closest to me, than anyone else. The worst thing was seeing my mom's heart beaten down and exposed, scarred and battered, and watching her collapse into oblivion.

Chapter Four

ONCE WHOLE NOW BROKEN

"Mom, Mom, are you OK?"

I barely caught her as I eased her fall down to our wooden floor. Her eyes rolled back as if she was seizing or having a heart attack.

"Mom, do I call 911? Should I call Dad?"

She blinked at me, shaking her head no, as I gave all of myself to get her standing. Then I carried half of her weight to her bed.

"Let me get you to bed. Don't get up. I'll get you water."

I was so scared. My thoughts turned into cries for help, cries of hopelessness. *God, don't let her die from this. She's not eating. I don't know what to do.* Dying from a broken heart. I wouldn't wish this on anyone.

Suddenly, this broken family was experiencing the death of old memories of the glory days. The family unit we used to know died and was never resurrected. Once upon a time, my trust never wavered, but suddenly it seemed as though it'd been buried with my united family. Our once-upon-a-time was no fairy tale. We died to how things used to be. We died to our yesterdays without hope for tomorrow.

How do you breathe when your life source has sunk to the pit, where there is no light, knowing that with light there usually was hope? How do creatures live in the pit of the ocean floor, with its absence of light? If only I could come to a bit of light, just maybe I could learn to breathe again.

I prayed for my mom to breathe again. Seeing my mom gasping for air, crying for love, wishing for trust, I wondered if this would lead to divorce or separation, and even deeper loss. Could it get any worse than this?

Racing thoughts consumed me, thousands of thoughts per minute. I wondered where my dad was staying and if he had a whole other life or even another child. Every day, I wondered if he was ever going to love my mom again. I didn't know what love was supposed to look like, but I was seeing what love wasn't. This was the separation of love, two hearts ripping apart, a push and pull, yet each piece needed the other to function. How do you get the infected piece to rejuvenate?

———❧———

My days were spent wondering if the separation would become a divorce. Divorce is a great sin against God, except if one commits infidelity. My mom knew this and still loved my dad. How could she stay with him?

We spoke again shortly before she was taking a vacation to Barbados to see her mom. Dad wasn't around, and I asked her if they were going to stay together. Mom told me she was asking God what to do, and God said to stay with him because He will take care of us all. She trusted God and stayed with my dad, but she didn't know if he would go or not. She gave him the option to file for divorce, even though she was willing to try to fix their marriage.

Mom suggested marriage counseling through the church. He didn't want to do marriage counseling at the church because his view of the church was skeptical. He told my mom he didn't love her anymore, but he still decided to do counseling with her even though his love had run out.

Those words haunt me: *I don't love you anymore.* I don't just one day stop loving someone I've loved for years. My biggest fear began to sink in. I was afraid my dad would actually leave us, my mom would be a single mom with five kids, and I would be another stereotype.

These lies began to sit in my mind. I started to believe I wasn't good enough, worthy enough, or loved enough to keep my dad, especially if my mom wasn't enough for him. How could she not be? I thought I was special, Daddy's little princess, his Cinderella.

Discouragement and disappointment don't even compare to the despair in my heart. Maybe just like Cinderella I was meant to be a servant girl, all alone, in a dungeon, forgotten for no one to see, to know, or to care for and love. I lost my slipper that kept me on solid ground. I lost my reasons to take my next steps forward. I was a crying princess with her shoe left behind.

I knew I needed saving from this nightmare. Time didn't stop for me and my sorrow. Tomorrow was on its way.

Summer came to an end, and my journey to college began. I started studying athletic training and met a few people. Somehow I managed to put up a front that I was a regular girl who wasn't dying inside. I ended each night by crying and suppressing my feelings and fears. I started each morning with an alarm clock and a fake smile. I attended intro classes and got accustomed to each sports team, attempting to stay away from all soccer teams. Soccer reminded me too much of my reality at home, which seemed inescapable.

My thoughts of how things used to be at home overwhelmed me no matter how far I drove to school each morning. I stayed very busy, and my fake smile began to charm people, especially a charming prince. Andy was a soccer player and so cute, like Prince Charming. He was charming and enticing with his words. Sometimes he would even get me to smile or laugh genuinely.

Andy was a great distraction, an attractive one. He started to text me every day as a friend and classmate. Slowly we got closer, and he started inviting me to parties, which I said yes to every time instead of studying for class. I did anything not to go home and anything not to feel like a shadow of myself.

I soaked in every compliment from Andy. Flirting became fun and stimulating. I wasn't invisible to him. I actually enjoyed being around him. He always had a way of drawing me in with his smile and charm, but when we departed, I still seemed numb.

I was so innocent, soft-spoken, quiet, and seemed to not know who I was. I had felt so secure before all this happened with my family. I couldn't understand how this happened. Because of this, I was frustrated and then sad, but frustration felt a little bit more under my control.

I was easy to take advantage of because of the way I loved people and always gave all of myself. I was so genuine, never deliberately wanting to hurt a soul. I always restrained myself from causing pain to others, almost knowing in some way we were all hurting on the inside.

I had only five friends and coworkers in college. I remember feeling invisible every day. I felt so unknown, like I was dust, seen for a second and gone in the wind the next. No one wanted to know me. I was a shadow, this nice girl who never fit in or felt understood. I looked like them, but I didn't speak like them.

To them and the world, I was always put in a category of too white for black people, too properly spoken, too nice and sweet, and too smart. Why couldn't I just be seen and known for me, for who I was on the inside and not the color of my skin, my speech, my intelligence, my work, or how I looked? I never got too close to people. Loneliness started to become my identity.

Slowly, Andy wiggled his way into my world. He was consistent and seductive. Then, suddenly, I wasn't innocent anymore. With him I started to be more promiscuous, and that filled the numbness for a moment. But the numbness would come back, always quicker than the last time. At my lowest time, at least someone wanted me. I wasn't alone. I was noticed.

Yet I still never felt known by him, at least not sincerely, anyway. I walked around campus just trying to feel something. Every day I thought about the reason for all of this, the day it would all end. Would I ever be the same again? *Just keep walking,* I told myself, *just keep breathing.*

I started to sleep at Andy's, in my car, in my friend's dorm, anywhere. My home was the last place I ever wanted to be. If I had to go home, I went home hoping my dad wasn't there. I thought I'd had enough hurtful betrayal for a lifetime at this point, but no, there was more.

Chapter Five

CINDERELLA SURVIVING

Let me begin with Carrie and Caity, the only true joys in my life, the sisters who made me feel alive. They always loved me more than I loved myself. They always wanted the best for me, yet they never condemned me. Instead, they always told me that I deserved better. I always wanted to believe them.

I met Carrie my senior year of high school in New Jersey. She had moved from Massachusetts, and we instantly clicked at basketball tryouts. She was lovely, caring, and sweet, and I instantly knew she had a heart of gold. Somehow, I had to be her friend, and that was exactly what happened. Since that day I introduced myself, we've been best friends and forever will be.

Carrie always knew what to say to encourage me, console me, and comfort me, especially when life kept giving me wounds. Carrie was my escape, my truest friend, definitely a godsend. When Carrie was home from college, we spent every second together, inseparable. I poured my heart out to her, and she poured her heart out to me as we caught up with the latest details of our lives. We were home to each other, a different world, a safe and secure world of love. That family always brought me so much peace.

Because of Carrie, I got close to her sister, Caity. When Carrie was at college, Caity and I spoke all the time and would pass on the information to Carrie. They were the type of friends who stayed up all night with you during a hard time, friends who would blast music to dance and scream out of car windows. They were the type of friends who become your sisters. They were so special to me.

I would never talk about it, but Caity knew about my parents, and about the story with Andy. Caity never judged me for living a promiscuous life, and I always wanted to be pure like her. Their family became my world and my dream family. They all loved God, and I always thought *Wow, this is what a godly family looks like, this is what a godly marriage looks like.*

Caity's mother would tell me scriptures and things about God all the time. Even though Caity would have enough of her mom speaking about Jesus over and over, I was like a toddler soaking in every word. I desired to know more.

I slept over at their house most nights and most weekends to be with them, but also because their home was a safe haven for me that I never took for granted. Every holiday, birthday, and random gathering was at Carrie's house. I was always there with good news or terrible news. They became my second family, the family I chose, a family that chose me. These daughters became sisters I've always wanted, and their parents became images of the parents I wanted to be like someday.

They were always declaring the word of God. I desired a family like this, not perfect but set apart and filled with the love of God. Carrie and Caity were there for all parts of my life—the good, bad, and ugly. There were so many betrayals that led me back to the resentment, anger, and hopelessness my dad bestowed on our family by his actions.

There were so many special little moments I will never forget that actually saved my life in my hopelessness. Thank you, God, for those moments with Caity and Carrie, my loves, who stuck around closer than a brother ever could. Proverbs 18:24 says, "there are friends who destroy each other, but a real friend sticks closer than a brother." God sent me two sisters.

Caity was the sassy sweet rebel. She taught me over the years to speak my truth, like my aunt, no matter what. I love the fire in her heart. She is a loyalist to no end, always taking care of me and holding me tight. Caity has heard it all, everything I was proud of and everything I wasn't proud of. She never let me be ashamed or self-critical. She's my person who always lifts me up and always tells me the truth, even if it hurts. As Proverbs 27:5 says, "An open rebuke is better than hidden love."

I couldn't have asked for a better friend. She has really loved me unconditionally, and she isn't even family. Many nights I would cry in her arms, call her late at night, laugh with her for hours, and go on car-ride dates. My reasons for getting out of the house were bad, but Caity was a protective escape for me. I felt completely safe by her side. She has always been my ride or die.

In my eyes and my heart, Caity has basically been a perfect human. My prayer for her is that someday she can really see how important she is to so many people. I love her big eyes that tell you all about her. I love her big smile that makes you know everything is going to be OK. Most of all, I love her heart—her heart that leans on me and calls me friend. These are girls who can go anywhere in the world, but never anywhere so far that my love won't find them right where they are.

I'll never forget the night during Christmas break when I was at Caity's house enjoying their annual Christmas party and received a text message from one of my coworkers from school. She texted me a picture and a link to Andy's girlfriend's Instagram. I was shocked and so angry. Another liar and deceiver. I felt like I had a sign on my forehead saying, *Get with me if you are a cheater.*

Instantly in shock, I told all the girls what had happened. I apologized to his girlfriend on Instagram, picturing his girlfriend as my mom, who never deserved this pain. I felt so disgusting and ashamed for being in bed with deceit. It's ironic how I fell into the arms of the exact type of man I was running from at home.

I realized at that moment there's no escape from this type of life. I felt as though I should've known. I remember texting Andy the evidence, and I ignored his call as flames could have burst through my nostrils like a Leviathan. At that point, trust was something I didn't have anymore at all. I definitely lost another piece of my heart; my heart was bleeding out from multiple parts.

Numbness deepened in me. There was no way out. Caity and the girls comforted me that night as I told them more details of the story. They were proud of me for telling the truth and asking for forgiveness from his girlfriend. How could I face him at school? Somehow I was still surviving all of this.

It breaks my heart that someone can play games with hearts so well. A man can look at a girl and plan so much evil in his heart. I couldn't run from him. I had to run to sit next to other people so I wouldn't be able to see him gazing at me. I hated reality. When I would see Andy and his girlfriend pass through the Student Center where I worked, I avoided them at all costs. Every time I would see him or her, a traumatic jab to the heart had me shaking and trembling away from the scene.

I was a lone wolf at school, and I needed something to focus on. Working in college, and seeing Andy in my athletic training classes, wasn't working for me anymore. The temptation of being with him was so strong that I hated myself more. At some point, I knew I would fall in bed with him again if I stayed. I needed out.

—☙—

One day, I was home and devastated. My dad got off the phone with my uncle just before I was going to leave the house. He told me that nursing would get me a lot of money straight out of college and would give me work all my life. I thought about it on my drive to college, looked into it, and asked around. People said nursing was the hardest schooling next to a doctorate.

The difficulty of nursing didn't scare me away. I was more afraid of who I would become if I stayed. I needed the change, something to focus on, a way out of this torment. I was shocked that of all people, my dad gave me an out to be away from himself and Andy and Andy's girlfriend all at once.

So I applied to a nursing college, and I got in very quickly. This new journey gave my dad and I something to talk about after barely speaking for a year. I missed him, but I didn't like him anymore. I didn't trust him. I didn't respect him, but somehow I knew to listen to him, and he led me here.

This new journey was good for me. It gave me a fresh start and a new focus. My school life was hard and my family life was shattered, yet I preferred the hard over the shattered. At least school was something I could control, and it was on me, my efforts, my commitment. I could remain faithful to the very end. I could be trusted, wishing everyone else could be too.

—◆—

At this point, my parents were thinking about separating, after almost a year of marriage counseling. My mom told me that Dad needed to feel needed and wanted to provide for people. They were learning about each other's personalities and love languages at the church.

I didn't know how to feel when my parents sat all us kids down at the dining room table one morning. Dad wanted to discuss their marriage and what would happen with the family. The elephant in the room was large and agonizing. I looked at my oldest brother and saw that his heart was burdened. I looked at my youngest brother, one of the twins, and saw that he was questioning everything. I looked at the older twin and saw that his heart of innocence was changing. I looked at Mom and saw that her heart was shattered and her eyes were so sorrowful.

Then I looked at Dad, and I could tell his heart was almost unbothered and somehow still strong as he said, "All of you will be taken care of. I may not be around as much, but financially, everything will be the same. You will all be in the house with Mom."

I was holding back tears and screams, as though time had stopped like a blur. I had no control over any of it. My poor brothers; why did they have to grow up in this?

In my head I was contemplating life: *Nothing will be the same, Dad. Nothing has been the same for a year now. Nothing about this is OK.*

As I was screaming in my head, I wanted to tell him that *a dad is not just someone who provides financially, but provides love. I never wanted you to just give me things. I always just wanted you, Dad, just your heart, your love, and some care. I wanted you to never hurt me and to always tell me the truth. I love you, but I don't trust you, and I'm so disappointed in you. We don't deserve this!* But the words never ever came out. I wasn't strong enough.

—⊗—

I knew that everything happens for a reason and thought something good would come out of my failures and disappointments in life. I used distractions to get me through the day as I hoped that maybe one day things would get better. I tried to always forget the pain by staying busy, living for small things like getting a degree and helping my mom. I always wanted days to go faster, as if wishing for time to pass quicker would lead me to a better life or the chance to die faster.

My life was like a hamster's on a never-ending wheel, chasing my guilty pleasure, things that would make me feel alive for a few minutes. I let the desire for money, power, success, and even pleasure enter my world. I was so afraid to keep failing, to keep falling lower in depression, and to keep feeling broken and bruised. I felt like I had to build up walls to survive.

The feeling of time moving so fast and me getting nowhere was sickening. What was I here for? Who was I? What did I really want to do with my life? Where would I start? Was I ever going to feel wanted, needed? Would I ever be first in someone's eyes? I had many questions, many feelings, many fears, and many worries.

Maybe I was meant to be a magician, because I truly was one when it came to hiding my sadness and deepest, secret pain. People were still drawn to me, drawn to my fake smiles and fleeting happiness. Building up walls became a practice in my life, a career, until it became a way of life. The screaming and cries inside just grew and became louder in my head. I was a picture-perfect girl, attractive, educated, fit body, but dying inside.

Picture that girl who has always been very popular in school. She was always recognized, smiling all the time, at a party in a crowd of people where everyone is having a great time laughing, talking, drinking, smoking, and yet you'll never know that she felt so isolated, completely alone, just needing a shoulder to cry on. She got so good at not being OK. She was me. It was always surprising how I didn't break down in the middle of my whole life.

I wanted to be wanted and needed so bad, and to not be second. This Cinderella who lost her dad and herself was a girl screaming and kicking to find air. I was fighting to breathe, as if I was being buried alive, and as I got a little bit excited about life, more dirt got piled into my emptiness, into my grave.

I was just waiting for something or someone to make me whole again. I felt blind to beauty and deaf to hope. A life of thoughts and questions clouded my head every second. What am I missing, and how can I be happy?

This lost Cinderella began to write songs that captured her agony, journals of words that recorded her heart's cries, paintings of dreams that seemed unreachable, drawings and doodles that had no destiny. My letters I never sent to people were my only way of saying everything I wanted to say on paper that I couldn't say in person.

Most of my letters were to God. I wrote about things I wouldn't want to imagine and experiences I wouldn't want anyone to go through. I wondered if I was the only one who felt this way, like a ghostwriter, a princess who doesn't seem to exist. On August 31, 2015, I wrote, "The hardest thing about being a teenager is not knowing who you are or who you are supposed to be. Every day is a battle with yourself. Each day you are missing something within you, in your soul, in your life. What is that piece of emptiness?"

My journals reminded me of things in my childhood that used to happen to me, things I didn't understand, things that I knew were supernatural. Cinderella had a fairy godmother, but I had God. My journaling was somewhat scary, as my life fell closer and closer to the pit of darkness. I knew that with believing in God, evil came too.

Writing out deep things about my family and my life brought memories flooding in. The memories scared me but also helped me process all the things I was going through. I would get dreams, understand the atmosphere I was in, get strange feelings about spirits behind people, and see visions of the future, or that turned out to be correct about a person. I thought I had lost my mind being reminded of these things.

Chapter Six

SUPERNATURAL

Let me invite you into a few of these memories. Most of my friends were lost. We all were. Friends of mine were struggling with intrusive thoughts and signs of anxiety and depression. Some were even suicidal, and they would isolate themselves from me. At certain points, they would get angry with me and call me a bad friend. They started to push me away.

It broke my heart that they were attacking me, lying to me, messing around with guys who didn't love them, and pushing me away when I loved them. All I wanted to do was help, listen, and be a loyal friend.

I felt spirits a lot, which I didn't know were spirits at the time. I thought it was just intuition about someone's character. I felt familiar spirits a lot around people I deeply loved. I felt the spirit of suicide, the spirit of depression, the spirit of manipulation, and the spirit of isolation.

At the time, I didn't know how I knew these things or could recognize them. I told no one I could do this or that I would experience these supernatural things. My friends and I had been through a lot together, but most of all we'd had a lot of fun. Our friendships were filled with joy, laughter, love, and adventure— until they weren't. They all completely changed.

Another memory came in as I realized my best friends became acquaintances or even strangers as time passed. I learned over the years that love is painful, and loving is not easy. Love takes strength, courage, faith, and fight. Love is long-suffering because you still love someone even when they hurt you repeatedly. I began to see why Mom stayed with Dad through all the heartbreak, distrust, and turmoil.

Another memory of this spiritual gifting I never understood happened my senior year with my best friend, Lia. We were the closest, and we had a falling out because of a boy, and I felt mistreated.

I had a dream shortly after the falling out of friendship. In the dream, Lia and I were far apart in a cabin at a camp. We looked across the room and our eyes met. She began to cry as she came over to me to say she missed me and she was so sorry. The dream ended in reconciliation between us.

A few weeks later, the dream came true. Toward the end of senior year, Lia and I went to a peer leader retreat at a camp, just like the dream. I had no idea we would be going to a camp. It was like I had déjà vu when we were at the camp in the cafeteria and my eyes met hers across the room.

Unlike in the dream, I was the one who went up to her without thinking. I said, "Hi."

She said, crying, "Hi. I've missed you. I'm so sorry."

We hugged and cried, and we became friends again. I never told her about that dream.

Lia and I are not as close now because of distance due to college, but whenever we get a chance, we catch up. It was a beautiful thing that my mind stored up these pictures or dreams that told a story. Somehow I knew this would only be possible because of God.

I began to remember myself as a little girl, a little Cinderella, frightened from a nightmare that felt so real. I had so many nightmares that at the age of ten, I cried out to God, "Please stop me from dreaming. I'm scared!" And God answered this.

I continued to write all my experiences and flood of memories. I wrote letters to people I loved that I never gave to them, things I could never say out loud. I never wanted to hurt anyone with my feelings of how they hurt me deeply. I had a voice in my writing, but in reality, I was a silent little bird with clipped wings. I needed saving from falling, and I needed help learning how to fly. At least these letters were in my control and no one could take them away from me.

Finally, I wrote a letter to my dad:

Dear Dad,

I'm so hurt by your actions that not only broke my mom but broke me. Aside from God, you are my world, and the only person I could trust, love, and fully give my heart to. The last person I ever thought would break my heart was you. The man I love the most completely damaged my trust. I'm so scared to love, and so scared to experience this again. I'm hurt that you weren't thinking about your beautiful wife or children when you were doing wrong. I am trying, again and again, to let go of this disappointment, hate, and anger I have toward the choices you made. I want to replace these feelings with love and joy with all my heart. This betrayal, I can't bear. I still love you and I always will, but I just don't understand, and you never took the time to apologize and to explain.

I also wrote a letter to Mom:

Dear Mom,

God is the only one who could show you the way
through something like this. Dad's giving into
temptation is not your fault. You are so faithful,
it's beautiful. You are so strong, smart, more than
capable, more than enough, and very captivating.
I need you to try to believe these truths. It kills me
to see you go through this more than you will ever
know. I love you more than words can describe.
Psalm 119:28 says, "my soul is weary with sorrow;
strengthen me according to your word." Isaiah
40:31 says, "but those who hope in the Lord will
find new strength. They will soar high on wings
like eagles. They will run and not grow weary.
They will walk and not faint."

Before writing those letters years ago, all I wanted was to feel
OK again, to just breathe for a minute. I needed to feel like my
heart wasn't being torn into pieces every second. I wanted my
perfect world back. Matthew 10:39 says, "if you cling to your life,
you will lose it; but if you give up your life for me, you will find
it." Back then, I was clinging to my life, a life that was never mine
to own. I was so hurt and confused, with no idea how to get out.

My dad made a choice that blew up in his face and changed
all of us, and our relationships with him. He never protected his
family's hearts. He didn't realize that when his wife cried and
screamed, his daughter lamented in excruciating silence, and his
sons fumed with anger and pain. Innocence was lost. When his
wife hid in sorrow, so did his daughter.

His sons depended on me for everything during that time,
all types of information about our parents. I couldn't handle it.

The boys needed a dad to teach them how to love the right way. I was glad my younger brother wasn't home to experience what I experienced. I was glad my oldest brother was never home to witness anything. I hated that he would ask me how Mom was and what had been happening.

I hated it all because I was living in it and it was already tormenting my mind day and night. I never wanted to replay the arguments, the yelling, screaming, crying, fainting, and sadness in my mind over and over again.

I needed a way out, so I started running away. I would run outside for hours, run away anywhere to just not feel, think, or see the trauma in my head. Parties were perfect distractions, staying at school working helped, and taking late shifts kept me busy.

I would sleep in my friend Bell's dorm a lot at the time, whenever I wasn't home. I left the twins home to fend for themselves—well, mostly the older twin. I regret that still to this day. I should have been there for him, no matter how much it hurt me to be home. I know he remembers a lot of things from that time that he probably struggles with today.

During that time, I went into Protecting Mom mode. I would be her personal spy, which destroyed me more. I would send her texts when Dad would come and go, and for how long he would be out. I even checked his phone once for her when he was sleeping. All these things were so wrong and I felt that, so my only way out was to remain at college. I couldn't say no to my mom.

I commuted to college every morning if I didn't stay the night. I lost so much weight, just like my mom. I felt myself slipping away, becoming more numb by the day. I remember for years I only smiled at work, with Caity and Carrie, or when I was getting attention from boys. For a long time, I was the walking dead pretending to be alive. Bell went through something similar, but she was older and never wanted to talk about it with anyone.

I walked through the halls trying to find a space, a place to be heard, seen, and understood. When did my heart get so cold? I couldn't run away, as much as I tried to, because even though I wanted nothing to do with my dad or my life, I needed him and I needed to live. I needed a father's love, no matter how many times I tried to convince myself otherwise.

When you don't know who you are and whose you are, the enemy sweeps in to steal, kill, and destroy. Many questions remained unanswered, and many lost thoughts consumed me. I knew I needed saving.

Chapter Seven

GUARD YOUR HEART

Life continued to smack me in the face. Reality struck again, and it was time to go back to school and face Andy after he found out I told his girlfriend everything. He was mad, but I didn't care, so I sat somewhere else as I entered our kinesiology class. I ignored him for a while, even though he tried to talk to me. Eventually, I knew I would get over it, so I did and so did he.

He kept trying to talk to me, and I finally gave in and agreed to talk in his dorm room—a big mistake. I had to stay away from him, because my flesh was weak. I was officially a slave to sin.

Time passed, and I decided I needed a change. Before I transferred to nursing school, I asked a nurse practitioner, who would give me birth control throughout my first year and a half of college, about nursing. It was such a strange time—like, who gets a birth control shot while asking a nurse practitioner about her whole career and where I should go to school? I knew that, in a way, I was running away again rather than facing my pain. I knew God knew too. I was always running—running from my house, running from my dad, running from my mom, running from Andy, and running away from God. I wrote this poem:

I miss you D, how things used to be.
I miss you M, once a happy family.
I miss you S, glad you are not a witness to the mess.
I miss you A and you J, both so far away.
I miss you R, once upon a friend.
I don't want to miss you K. I want you, P, could be.
I need you, me. God save me.
Are you OK with sleeping now, me?

I wrote this poem because I was trying to fight to be all right. To be healed was what I wanted. At that time, Andy was still in my life, even though he really shouldn't have talked to me ever again knowing he was still with his girlfriend. Shameful and gross it was.

I told a few people at work about it all. I confided in them a lot, just because guys understand guys. I wished I would just allow myself to hurt instead of running from guy to guy who would just continue breaking my heart over and over again. I wish I knew then that the only man I ever needed was the Lord! For so long, I was supposed to "seek the kingdom of God above all else, and live righteously, and he will give you everything you need," as it says in Matthew 6:33.

Before I started nursing school, I still sought an escape and not God. Instead of seeking God, I booked a trip with Bri and Val to Punta Cana. I had so many fun, risky adventures with the twins. I love them so much.

Bri comforted me a lot when I would have breakdowns at work, when the toddlers were sleeping during naptime or my lunch breaks. Whenever life was less busy, I would have many hard days, because the silence led to bad thoughts, sad thoughts about everything going on. I worked every day of the week, and

I broke down in tears around the same time every day. I wished I didn't feel everything so deeply.

I suffered from broken pieces. I suffered from unexpected tragedies. Experiencing these struggles in my life led me to never measure or compare people's pain because everyone is made very differently, and pain is pain. Some pains are quick sufferings and others are long sufferings. Love suffers long! I knew this firsthand for four years, and sometimes even now I realize God is still mending some pieces. Purification is not a one-time deal, but God purifies perfectly.

Revelation 21:4 says, "And God will wipe away every tear from their eyes; there shall be no more death, nor sorrow, nor crying. There shall be no more pain, for the former things have passed away." I wanted that. No more sorrow, and all my tears wiped away.

God blessed me with friends I never asked for. Bri was going through similar stuff at the time. She held me tight, and ever since then, those sisters have shown me love, creativity, and parts of the world's beauties. We've seen sunsets, mountains, rivers, valleys, and far-off beaches. We've shared many scary, beautiful moments together. They were always so talented, but they didn't realize it, nor did they believe me when I said it. They never understood that the doubts in their heads were from the enemy telling them lies, but neither did I.

So because we were so close, we all decided to go on vacation to Punta Cana, and it was exactly what I needed. This place was stunning. And apparently I was stunning to one of the workers at the resort. Sometimes the things or people you think are good and perfect for you are the exact opposite of perfect for you. People in the world may look good and nice, but once their real identity is exposed, you see the liars, cheaters, stealers, and destroyers.

It was May 22, 2018, when I thought I was healed, new, free, and more beautiful. I thanked God for His blessings every day, even the ones in disguise. I thought God threw Jesse in the mix of my life to be a good thing, even though together we *weren't* a good thing, God had us meet for a reason, or so I believed.

Before I went to Punta Cana, I felt broken and needed healing from all of life's gunshots. There was Andy, who I shared all the wrong feelings and impulses with. There was Dad, who I was trying to forgive. There was Mom, who was not soothing me, but wanted too. It was as if I finally felt God's warmth in the sun, the water, Jesse's smile, his contagious laugh, and the curiosity he made in me.

God is love, and He works everything for our good. Romans 8:28 says, "And we know that all things work together for good to those who love God, to those who are called according to His purpose."

Jesse was chivalrous, always treating me, a stranger, like a princess. At the resort, we started to spend so much time together throughout the trip. Quickly, a lot of sexual sin took place with us. It all seemed new and exciting. I knew this would be something short-lived from the start, but I didn't want it to be.

I would compare him to Andy all the time—sexually, physically, and emotionally—especially when he would want to talk to me alone, away from my friends. I was so naive. He hated when I would tell him "maybe" or "I don't know" when he asked me to date him. I knew he was a sweet sensitive guy, but I also knew it wouldn't last no matter how hard we tried.

I would contemplate whether we could have a future together, wanting him to love God so much that he would believe God sent him to me, and to know that God makes no mistakes. I wanted so badly to add him to my future; I even started talking to him about ways to come visit me in the US sooner rather than later.

Once all the fun died, like the partying and drinking, Jesse and I spoke on the phone almost every day until it was time for us girls to go back home. The twins and I went home after two weeks. Right away, I wanted to see him again. I fell in love with the idea of a fairy-tale exotic story about him and I living in Punta Cana for a little while to figure things out. Little Cinderella was hoping for a fairy-tale ending, one that would never come.

I settled in at home and told my mom and dad about him because I was starstruck and naive. I started sending him money to try to get him to visit me. I even tried asking my parents about how he could come visit. They were shocked but didn't turn down the wild thoughts I was having. I wanted it to be like my mom and dad, how their long-distance relationship worked before the whole scandal happened.

I even thought about marrying the guy, like farm girl and city boy. Young love really was lust in my circumstance. At least I asked God for clarity and perspective, and the push to visit him, but that push never came, and phone calls became distant memories.

Over time, staying connected became more and more difficult. I knew I had started to hurt him. Then one day, he showed me a new tattoo he got when he was supposed to be saving to come visit me in the states. Right after he sent me that picture, I knew I was getting played. I felt so foolish and angry.

When I began to sin, especially began living and practicing sexual sin, all the other evil things I swore I would never do in my life, I eventually started to do. I was so messed up. I did the very thing I hated out of anger and feelings of betrayal. I became a hypocrite.

I ended up cheating on Jesse with a coworker at the restaurant I worked at before I decided to break up with him officially. I truly became everything I hated. Sin and shame were not just in my world but they were *from* me. *I* was the problem. So who was I to not forgive my dad and others? Who was I to not ask for God's mercy? How could I not repent and ask for God's mercy? Isaiah 63:7-14 is titled *God's Mercy Remembered*:

> I will mention the lovingkindnesses of the Lord
> and the praises of the Lord, according to all that the

Lord had bestowed on us, and the great goodness toward the house of Israel, which He has bestowed on them according to His mercies, according to the multitude of His lovingkindnesses. For he said, "Surely they are My people, children who will not lie." So he became their Savior. In all their affliction He was afflicted, and the Angel of His presence saved them; In His love and in His pity He redeemed them, And He bore them and carried them all the days of old. But they rebelled and grieved the Holy Spirit, so He fought against them. Then He remembered the days of old Moses and his people, saying "where is He who brought them up out of the sea with the shepherd of His flock. Where is He who put His Holy Spirit within them, who led them by the right hand of Moses? With His glorious arm, dividing the water before them to make for Himself an everlasting name, who led them through the deep, as a horse in the wilderness that they might not stumble?" As a beast goes down into the valley and the Spirit of the Lord causes him to rest, so You lead Your people to make Yourself a glorious name.

Sometimes as sinners, we forget who saved us time and time again. God saved us every time we turned our backs on Him. He had mercy on me who couldn't forgive my dad for doing something so disgusting, an evil act that I did as well. God knows His people; some go astray, but He still knows His people, "children who will not lie ... So He became their Savior." This I want to be, a child who does not lie. I hated that my dad lied. I wish I was different, a better person.

I wanted to believe God didn't only give us truth, mercy, goodness, security, love, redemption, and many loving-kindnesses, but He also gave us saving grace. The Holy Spirit is placed within us if we confess with our mouths and believe in our hearts that Jesus is Lord. God also tells us about His power when He remembers the old days when He split the sea and led Moses to guide the people through the deep. He protected them in the wilderness, even from the things they didn't see, like the beast in the valley. God's name is glorious!

So next time I think I did nothing wrong, and I don't want to repent, I pray I reread this verse and let this forever sink in and change my heart. God wants and loves a repentant heart. I wish I opened my heart to the God of the universe, Jesus. I didn't understand anything about the Holy Spirit. I continued in sin, grieving the Holy Spirit, not knowing the Holy Spirit had my best interest in mind.

After three months of battling with the sin and shame of cheating, I ended things with Jesse, even though he forgave me for cheating. Andy continued to text me and add me on Snapchat and Instagram just to keep me tied to him like a rag doll. I realized I was lying to myself thinking I had let him go. This soul tie had me chained—a soul tie I had no idea about, one I didn't know could be broken by Christ.

During that time, I made a promise to God to stop fornicating because I felt convicted every time I was reading the Bible, every time I tried to get closer to God. I knew I couldn't be living in sin and be connected to God at the same time because God is so Holy. He knew I loved sin and that He was the only one who could save me enough to hate sin. God knew I desired Him, but I couldn't repent and couldn't allow such a Holy God in my heart to capture it, at least not yet. How could such a Holy God love me? I didn't even love myself.

Soul-shattering repentance was needed in me, and complete

surrender had to have full reign over my heart and mind. God doesn't force himself into our hearts; instead, He gives us free will to choose to love Him and live for Him. A dictator loves himself, not his people. God laid down His life selflessly because He loved His people. God isn't a dictator but a Father and Friend.

Free will is the reason we keep choosing to live in sin. It is because we love to sin more than we love God. We don't understand. Once we realize how much God really loves us even when we hate ourselves, only then will we know the power in the crucifixion and resurrection of Jesus. God gave His only begotten son to die on the cross for our sins and then defeated the death, hell, and sin that so easily ensnare us. Now all people have access to God, can have a loving relationship with God, and can have the Holy Spirit living within them if they receive Christ Jesus with their mouth and believe in their heart.

I was still a slave to sin. I didn't even trust my earthly father, so in my mind I thought, *How can I trust one I can't see? How will I know if He cares for me?* I thought my dad cared for me and my family, but there was betrayal and lies. I wanted the truth.

Romans 10: 8-13 says:

> The word is near you, in your mouth and in your heart [that is, the word of faith which we preach]: that if you confess with your mouth the Lord Jesus and believe in your heart that God has raised Him from the dead, you will be saved. For with the heart one believes unto righteousness, and with the mouth confession is made unto salvation. For the scripture says, "Whoever believes in Him will not be put to shame." For there is no distinction between Jew and Greek, for the same Lord over all is rich to all who call upon Him. For whoever calls on the name of the LORD shall be saved.

Hosea 4:6 says:

> My people are destroyed for lack of knowledge.
> Because you have rejected knowledge, I also will
> reject you from being priest for Me, because you
> have forgotten the law of God, I also will forget
> your children.

I knew nothing of this Father in heaven. I kept disobeying God and doing evil in His eyes. Judges 3:12-14 says:

> And the children of Israel again did evil in the
> sight of the Lord. So the Lord strengthened Eglon
> king of Moab against Israel because they had done
> evil in the sight of the Lord. Then he gathered to
> himself the people of Ammon and Amalek, went
> and defeated Israel, and took possession of the
> City of Palms. So the children of Israel served
> Eglon king of Moab eighteen years.

I was living in sin and truly lost myself at the age of eighteen years old. I was living in sin, cheating on God, cheating on the one who truly loved me all my life! I was living for Satan instead of living for my Creator, who is perfect and holy.

God is speaking to you, so seek God, because no one, no one loves you as Jesus does. Don't be so afraid, God will keep you safe.

Just because I was suffering didn't mean I wasn't blessed with much to be thankful for. Even though I was lost, God wanted to find me where I was, and He wanted to show me His love through the little joys that were actually big joys in disguise. For me, seeing my dad laugh with so much joy every time he played soccer or talked about old times with his brother was a big joy. Hearing my dad talk about all the excitement in New York City and telling us all about what his job was like with rats and roaches would always be hilarious. My dad's stories were epic and full of unimaginable experiences, childhood memories, and even moments of seeing evil spirits and hearing the voice of God say, "Don't do it."

God saved my dad's life many times. Seeing my dad's smile made me smile even though our relationship hasn't been restored. I love my dad so much, and it hurts to know he hasn't surrendered his life to God, as if he holds a grudge against Him or holds resentment of some kind in his heart.

And I still had resentment in my heart toward my dad. I wanted to reconcile, but I didn't know how. I missed having a healthy respectful relationship with my dad, but I still felt so betrayed and abandoned. So I continued to write letters to Dad that only God could read:

Dear Dad,

I forgive you, Dad, and I am sorry for resenting you. I am sorry for ignoring you, rolling my eyes, for cutting you off and being disrespectful. I am sorry for not considering your feelings. I am sorry for not realizing the love and words of affirmation you needed to feel loved, honored, and needed.

Dad, I am here to tell you how proud I am to be your daughter. My love for you will continue for generations. The only reason I was hurt so bad is because of how much I love and cherish you as my dad. I couldn't have asked for a better dad even with your faults and all. You are so gifted in everything you do, it astonishes me every day. Your laugh is contagious, and your goofiness brings me joy. I love when you sing and dance; my heart jumps because I love what you love. But Dad, if this is a love letter for you, Jesus loves you.

Just imagine what Jesus personally wants to say to you if you just let Him.

I repent, Lord; forgive me for not doing this sooner. Help me to love him profoundly because of all the years I haven't. Matthew 19:19 says, "honor your father and your mother; and you shall love your neighbor as yourself." Parents are a gift from God, so we must cherish them. It's hard loving someone who hurt us, so I've asked God to help me love again.

Dad, I am so sorry for the times I made you think I didn't love you. I could hug you forever if it was possible. Know that you are noticed. I see your heart and, most importantly, God sees your heart. Forgive me for not forgiving you.

Love, Brielle.

I kept reading my Bible every once in a while. As time passed, sin was still very present in my life. I couldn't stop even though I wanted to so badly. I wanted to stop feeling so empty after being with Andy, but I wasn't tired enough of it all to really stop. I continued to get sad, angry, anxious, and convicted. I even started going on dating websites as if that was a good idea. I was struggling to love myself still.

———

My dad was home somehow sticking around, and I was still in college, almost done with nursing school. Confusion was still at the center of my life, along with loneliness and weakness. I felt condemned, and I didn't want to go all the way with this new Tinder guy.

I kept talking to guys and I met Zeke, this Spanish guy who

I found very attractive and honestly out of my league. Somehow, he wanted to be with me. We would smoke, talk, and hang out late at night.

I was deceiving myself, because I thought not going all the way with a guy was keeping my promise to God to stop living in sexual sin. I didn't understand that all sorts of sexual sin is sin, and doing a little was still doing everything in God's eyes. I believed a lie from the enemy that kept me bound. 1 Timothy 1:9-11 says:

> The law is not made for a righteous person, but for the lawless and insubordinate, for the ungodly and for sinners, for the unholy and profane, for murderers of fathers and murderers of mothers, for manslayers, for sexual immorality, for homosexuals, for kidnappers, for liars, for perjurers, and if there is any other thing that is contrary to sound doctrine, according to the glorious gospel of the blessed God which was committed to my trust.

Zeke was the most attractive guy I ever talked to, but he always kept me at arm's length, and he had very long arms. I was also trying to feel something with him, but emotionally I felt like he hated me, and mentally I felt like he was really confused about me. I didn't know what he wanted in his life. He had no direction. I continued to lie to myself, to God, and to Zeke about my true feelings.

Forgive me, God. I was running away from my true identity when I was supposed to be running toward my Father in heaven, to You. I was like the prodigal daughter running away from the loving Father who has His arms wide open to embrace me with love. I was thinking my Father in heaven wanted nothing to do with me because of my circle of sin, but that was a lie too. Jesus killed sin when He died on the cross, so running into the Father's arms is exactly what I should have done with all my baggage, all my brokenness, all my pain, all my tears, all my burdens, and all my sin.

I was hurt by Zeke because of his rudeness and the games he played, which led to my own disappointments continuing. I thought we were friends, but we weren't at all. In some ways, it was worse being with him than it was with Andy. I was actually really good friends with Andy before we started messing around. They both used me, though, for their own desires. They both deceived me because I was already deceiving myself.

I stopped seeing Zeke after he stood me up one day. I'd had enough. He apologized shortly after, but I knew he was only trying to get back on my good side to play with my heart again. I pray that Zeke and Andy both experience God's love for them. I bless them with all my heart, and I forgive both of them.

—◦◦◦—

Looking back, I've noticed that through all of my brokenness, I always had a small, very small amount of faith and hope. I always knew I was meant to live for something greater than myself. I always knew I couldn't give up because the people I was meant to touch would never be found, seen, or heard. The times I couldn't get out of bed and the countless nights crying myself to sleep, this voice in my head was always saying, *Sustain it, sustain it, people need you.* It was my personal race of faith, a race to an unknown finish line, a race that I would get beat up on, a race I wanted to quit.

This has always been a race of faith that was never meant for just my own gain but for others, too. Hebrews 12:1-2 says:

> Therefore we also since we are surrounded by so great a cloud of witnesses, let us lay aside every weight and the sin which so easily ensnares us,

and let us run with endurance the race that is set before us, looking unto Jesus, the author, and finisher of our faith, who for the joy that was set before Him endured the cross, despising the shame and has sat down at the right hand of the throne of God.

God gave me faith, especially when my hope was shaken.

After Zeke, I took breaks and I kept trying to stay away from sin, but I knew I was still missing God, as if my eyes made me blind to God's mercies and my ears made me deaf so I could not hear God's call for me. Matthew 13:15 says:

For the hearts of these people have grown dull. Their ears are hard of hearing, and their eyes have closed, lest they should see with their eyes and hear with their ears, lest they should understand with their hearts and turn so that I should heal them.

Chapter Eight

SLAVERY

Guys continued to be in my life. I thought these guys could love me and fill the void I'd been feeling. I wanted someone to protect me and my heart. These are natural things for a girl to want and need, but a worldly guy would never fill that void. Only God fills all voids.

I also yearned for my father so much, but I could never get myself to tell him just how much I needed him and would always love him deeply. I see a lot of sadness from my dad and my mom. I know they both have a lot of sadness from childhood that grew into their adulthood. Letters were easier for revealing my heart than speaking to the letter's recipient. I could hide behind the paper. I could hide from my dad, but never God.

Dear Dad,

God left the 99 for just you, one heart, one soul. You may think you are alone and in a fight you can't win, but the truth is you were never alone; you chose to be. You won't win this fight because you are fighting without Jesus. Jesus already fights for you behind the scenes in your life, but He wants to fight side by side with you.

Matthew 18:20 says: "For where two or three are gathered together in My name, I am there in the midst of them." God isn't against you; He is for you. He made your strong almond eyes so detailed with amber, that tiny crease near your eyes to form only one small portion of your contagious smile, those crooked teeth that helped you whistle for me and cheer me on in soccer. Those scars that tell a story, tell *your* story, Dad.

Feel your story, love your story, and then let go, and let God be the author and finisher of your faith, of your story. A story of a future walking with the Lord. A peaceful and prosperous story I declare for your life, in Jesus's name. Hebrews 12:5-6 says, "My son, do not despise the chastening of the Lord, nor be discouraged when you are rebuked by Him; For whom the Lord loves He chastens and scourges every son whom He receives."

Love, Brielle

For a while, I continued to push on through it all. I needed a father who loved me, one who would not just protect me physically and financially but protect my heart and soul. I didn't know if I was beautiful. *You never told me, Daddy.* I didn't know if I was worth it. *You didn't fight for me.* I didn't know I could be loved unconditionally. *You didn't love Mom unconditionally, so how could I know? I'm just a child, Daddy, how could I know? How do I know who I am if I'm such a burden for you? I do all this so you will be proud, but nothing satisfies you.*

Nursing school was so hard, but it was nothing compared to the turmoil in my heart and mind. *I can't survive this any longer,* I always thought. There were fights in my home life, with awkward talks about their thoughts of separation or divorce. There were many men on my phone constantly, and there were my own insecurities and internal frustrations. I was partying with Beth while feeling empty, but trying to force myself to have fun, and alcohol made it easier to do that. Beth and I also worked out a lot, but I always felt lonely.

Beth was a girl who wanted to be loved just like the rest of us but looked for it in the wrong places, like I did. We ended up being that way together. Beth was always so beautiful and outgoing that she would speak to absolutely anyone. I always admired that about her. Jesus wants her to know Him for this reason and for many more reasons, for purposes that will bring her peace, joy, and love. I pray that Beth realizes whose she is and truly accepts Jesus into her heart as her Savior, Friend, and Father. Amen!

Through Beth, I met Landon, this cute blond with mysterious blue eyes. He was the definition of a mystery to me. I could never figure out who he was. I don't even think he knew.

That relationship was filled with confusion. We were both confused as to who we were. I feel like Landon and I were two lost souls who collided. I think he thought he couldn't truly be loved by anyone, so he kept people far from his heart. He had many cravings, ones he thought could fill the voids, fill the lies.

Landon was younger than me by about two years but was working in the city making a lot of money, living in his own apartment, and smoking every day. He would always reek of smoke without knowing the smoke would sometimes provoke my asthma. He smoked so much, like it was his food.

I can't understand how I ended up with someone so strung out. He loved partying and booze, and lazy days watching police shows. He loved my features and would tell me how beautiful and smart I was. I would tell him about God and ask him questions about his faith and what it was like living in Florida. He said he wanted to come to church with me but never did.

Just like the rest, Landon hurt me. He broke my trust by

sending a video of me to a friend—a friend I later associated myself with in more promiscuous ways. After that with Landon, I got more numb, and I started to really avoid my feelings again. I would forgive him and pray that all the voids he tried to fill he would give to God, repent, and have a full loving life.

At this time in my life, I knew men were my idols and seeking love was my addiction, like cheating was Dad's, and like lying was for so many of us. It was a vicious circle of false gods with empty, quick pleasures. Men kept me away from God. I kept myself from God.

I chose to try to let these men satisfy me, try to love me. I thought maybe they could show me the true meaning of love. Because of my home life, I allowed myself to be lost. The ways of men were my stronghold. Chasing guys kept me away from seeking a true relationship with God.

I needed them, I thought. My heart deceived me into thinking I needed the attention, the adoration, the validation. What I really needed was the love that only God could give, the validation of being God's child, the peace God always wanted to give me.

My hope was shattered. My heart was trampled, torn, and abused over and over again. Jeremiah 17:9 says, "The heart is deceitful above all things, and desperately wicked; who can know it?" I am wondering why I even took a break from guys if I was going to go back and make the same mistakes again.

Right after Landon, the next guy I also met through Beth was Jake, the rapper. You would think I'd have learned my lesson to never get with Beth's guy friends after Landon, but no. Jake rapped about me before he even got to know me. I thought it was really funny. I remember thinking I hoped he could use his talents someday to rap about the Lord, because he was always really good.

Jake was younger than me, immature and foolish. Caity would always tell me I would allow these guys in my life who were never worthy of me. I believed her, but I didn't know how to stop. Not every guy used me, but there were guys I used too.

Before Jake, there was a guy named Ben. He was so into me, but again, I was so unhealthy, with way too much baggage. I got so much attention from him, and that was why I let him hang out around me a lot of the time. He always wanted to please me, even though I didn't find him attractive. I just wanted a friend, and he didn't understand that.

Forgive me, Lord, for participating in acts and dependency that weren't good for me. I pray and rebuke all tendencies that are not of God by the blood of Jesus, Amen!

My false need for anything and anyone was so bad that I had no self-control, no self-worth, and no realization that I was hurting other people too. My numbness was pitch black, deep, and spreading, almost never-ending for years. Thinking about it all makes me so sad. There are so many young girls living lives like this. I needed someone to lean on, and I needed someone to slap me out of it, to lift me up.

I know now that God was always there holding me up with His right hand, so I wouldn't die. Eventually, I needed to allow Him into my heart fully. Isaiah 41:13 says, "For I the LORD your God, will hold your right hand, saying to you, fear not, I will help you." He was always there in every storm, every tear, and seeing every sin, waiting to snatch me out. When I was ashamed of myself, Jesus was there right with me, hating shame but loving me. The loving Father wants the best for His children. God made women for intimacy and security.

I remember growing up with my four brothers always doing what they wanted to do, never doing what my heart wanted. Even as a little girl, I wanted to feel safe and loved, and to be heard. Being the only girl was very lonely at times. Maybe that's why I always struggled with loneliness and latched onto friends and guys.

I don't have much memory of affection from my parents other than the bare minimum. With foreign parents, when things happen, you always take care of things by yourself. But what is the point of life if you are forced to live it alone? As people, we aren't meant to be alone.

Intimacy was something I always craved. Physical touch was always a need for me, a need never fulfilled. I realized that I never saw my parents really show each other love or affection when I was growing up. Affectionate touches seemed unnatural for them. If they kissed, it was a peck once in a while. There was never a compliment given to each other. I thought maybe they were only showing love in private, in secret, behind closed doors.

Mom was always very reserved, very quiet, and very particular with everything. She was raised by her mom, my gorgeous and amazing grandma, and my grandma's dad. My mom's real dad didn't watch her grow up. He was an alcoholic. So I couldn't imagine what her life was like without a dad around.

She talks about Great-Grandpa a lot, though, and the experiences she had with him on the plantation in Barbados. My mom lived on the wealthier side of town because my great-grandpa was a white Englishman who owned property in different areas of Barbados. Intimacy must have been a foreign act in her household too. Her only form of a dad was her grandpa.

On the other end of the spectrum, Dad grew up with both of his parents. He is very close with his older brother, and he had a lot of unimaginable things happen in his life spiritually with all his siblings. He told me his dad worked a lot to make ends meet, and his mom was a tough woman.

It seems that physical love and intimacy may not have been normal for either of my parents. They each have their own baggage that I think they still hold in their hearts—hearts they haven't shared with me, or with God.

I realized I never knew what love really was because maybe my own parents didn't either. Do any of us know the meaning of love? And if we don't know the true meaning of love, how can we give it or show it?

My dad provides, supports, and protects us physically. Mom took care of us and worked sometimes to help the family as well. I know working was something my mom never wanted, and honestly, neither did I, but my dad always instilled in me to never depend on a man to take care of me, and to always make my own way in the world, to be strong.

Mom had us kids soon after coming to this country, so her economic dependency had to be on Dad. She always engraved in my head to live life so you don't have to depend on a man to take care of you and your children. She wished she had gone to school and gotten a degree so Dad would stop nagging her about working again. If she didn't work at a job that stressed her out, I know she would have a creative studio to do what she was put here on earth to do: create with her anointed hands.

God is an artist, and so is my mom. God is an author, and so am I. He made us in His image. My dad is a strong worker, so much so that he could have been a Marine, a firefighter, or even made all kinds of things with his hands.

God has a purpose for each and every one of us. If my dad really knew Jesus and walked in authority and identity in Christ, I could see him evangelizing and doing missionary work all over the world preaching the Gospel, the Good News. Jeremiah 29:11 says, "For I know the plans I have for you declares the Lord they are plans for good and not for disaster. To give you a future and a hope."

Chapter Nine
PURPOSE

Purpose is the point of living. Why are you here? What are you called to do? What is that deep desire that seems so impossible? A purpose involves other people. Are you very self-absorbed? How could you change the world to look like heaven? How could you change someone's life to get a taste of how good God is?

Mark 10:27 says, "But Jesus looked at them and said, 'With men it is impossible, but not God; for with God all things are possible." I couldn't see anything being impossible because of my faith. I thank God for my faith, even though I still didn't have a genuine relationship with Him. I continued to struggle with my self-worth and identity. I couldn't see a light at the end of the tunnel.

Every day, I wondered if I would stop feeling so empty, if I would be in a crowd of people and continue to have no true, real, loving connections. Every guy I met kept himself at a distance. All conversations were shallow and surface. It was as if everyone in the whole world desired to be known and seen but were too scared to be seen for their true selves.

People only want people to see what's beautiful, but I've learned that only from ugliness can the most beauty arise. Ugliness has to surface so the beauty can be found. I could see this in all the guys I was with and mostly from my dad.

Jake was someone I got with because I didn't know how to be alone or my purpose in singleness. I just floated around like a dandelion, jumping around, and landing with some random guy. These guys were talkative, adventurous, creative, and determined about frivolous success. Mostly, all of them were hooking up with me and someone else too, similar to the Andy situation. I ended up giving up on my deep want to restrain from premarital sex.

To be safe, I went as far as getting an IUD because I gave up and knew I wasn't going to just stop sinning at this point. I was weak, and I was tired of fighting. The day I got it I went to sleep over at Caity's house while Carrie was still in school. I walked into the kitchen to only stand because the pain was still so unbearable and uncomfortable. I hadn't been completely warned about how painful the insertion would be.

I told Caity everything that took place at the doctor and with Jake. He had no idea I was getting an implant, yet somehow he texted me saying, "I don't want to be with you anymore because it is unfair to you." He told me how much of a great person I was and how he didn't want to use me. Right after this, he blocked me on all social media platforms and never answered my texts.

I don't know how I survived so much of this kind of treatment. I did all this stuff to be with him, and I wanted to keep doing what we were doing, because it was the way I received instant intimacy, pleasure, and a quick fix to fill the void. I was wanted in those moments. It was the closest thing to intimacy I'd ever received.

After he told me that, I was devastated and felt like I really wasted my time. I couldn't understand how the exact day I took protective action he texted me, ending it. God was protecting me from so much that day. I knew Caity knew that too. I believe God knew I wouldn't have stopped at all with Jake, because I stopped trying to live right, and I liked it too much at this point, even though I felt shame and guilt every time. Because of this, I told myself I might as well just continue to commit sexual sin, because obviously I couldn't stop.

God made sure Jake denied me. That was the first time a guy denied me. I praise God for that rejection, because I know I could have ended up pregnant or hurt worse if we continued.

I deleted him off my Snapchat and Instagram after he blocked me. Words can't even describe the angst and agitation in my heart after that. Somehow, the next guy always came like kryptonite. I was a jaded girl with daddy issues.

I was still in nursing school when my friend Jace began texting me more and more, though I had left our job at the Student Center. I always thought he saw me just as a coworker and friend. He had a girlfriend he really liked, but for some reason he was still interested in me.

I always loved Jace because his personality was very attractive to me. I loved his determination, friendship, and leadership. He was a great friend in college, but once I left, he started to drop hints that he was into me. Even though I was always into him from the moment I met him, I never thought he would be interested in someone like me. But honestly, I thought the same thing about Zeke years ago. I guess I was prettier than I thought.

Jace and I started to meet up and play basketball together at the gym near my house. We started texting, flirting, and confiding in each other. I didn't feel lonely anymore because I was getting attention again and talking to an old friend. I had to deny doing anything with him, though, because he had a girlfriend.

I told him all the time that he had to talk to his girlfriend and be honest because everything reminded me so much of my home life. Jace knew about my family and came over a few times, meeting my mom and brothers. I was so oblivious to his affection for me. It made me wish I knew my worth. I think he truly would have done so much for me.

All my relationships with men were really sad, if you

haven't noticed. I'm surprised I didn't hate men after all this. It's unbelievable, because Jake (the rapper), Andy, and Jace still add me back on Snapchat to see if I will accept their requests. They would always try to make their way back into my life. Jace would still text me with the same motives. Landon has tried getting back in my life multiple times. Zeke tried once. Ben saw me last at his job when my family was at the restaurant.

——

All of 2018 and the beginning of 2019 were consumed with the same sin and the need for saving. It had been about two years since my dad started cheating, and somehow he was still at home. My house was getting quieter every year. But my dad was still there. He stayed.

I had to keep my worlds separate. I had to pretend to be OK. Guys kept coming into my life. Attention and pleasure from men was the only affection I knew, so it was all I was determined to keep.

I went on some dates with a Navy man, Dan. He was a strong dark-haired lean-bodied type, white with light brown eyes, and very smart. He'd lived many places for his active duty. He would open up about his personal life with other girls way more than I would have liked. Where your heart is leads your life.

I realized I was very bored with Dan, because dates and conversation were boring for me. I didn't feel connected with him because we never talked about anything I liked to talk about. There was also no flirting or teasing, with jokes toward each other. He was into facts and psychology, politics, and pleasures, of course.

Later on, I called Caity and spazzed out because I felt like I should have known that he hadn't moved on from his past relationship. I knew he was still heartbroken over another woman. I was there for him as a listening ear, but in my brain I was like,

Oh my goodness, I am not just the side-piece but the second choice.
Eventually, I ended things because I just wasn't interested. He
was very upset and unkind over text, treating me like I was some
stranger on the street.

I was so devastated by my whole existence. I really felt
defeated, like I couldn't do this anymore. I couldn't help but think
something was seriously wrong with me that this stuff just kept
happening. *Can this life end?* I wondered. I was just so tired, and
this thought kept popping up. I wondered if I had to turn into a
mean girl and demand what I wanted to everyone I came across
to really be treated right and with respect and love.

During the time I talked to Dan, I was texting Landyn, but I
wasn't interested in Landyn like that. I was just lonely and wanted
someone to talk to. We'd met on social media and had mutual
friends from high school, but he was older than me. He told me he
was also a Christian, but we really weren't at all, because we were
both still living sinful lives, going against God's will. He left a bad
taste in my mouth, so I tried to just stop texting him. Then I just
ignored him because he wouldn't stop messaging me.

He texted me months later about going on a real date because
he liked me, but the whole time he was talking to other girls and
going on dates with them. I let him down as gently as I could that
Christmas when I was in Florida. He was a nice guy, but I wasn't
attracted to him, or interested in him either. I realized how terrible
it was that I ignored him instead of just saying a long time ago
from the very beginning that I didn't want to text him anymore.

Lonely and fragile, I seemed all the time a damsel in distress,
a very lost Cinderella, who could never get the love she needed.
There's this wallowing void when you have daddy issues. I'm so
sorry for all the girls and guys who feel this type of pain. Thank
God that Jesus went through all we have so that He could redeem
our broken stories.

Matthew 15:24 says, "I've got my hands full dealing with the
lost sheep of Israel." That was me, the lost sheep, and honestly,

so were all those guys in my life. But God waited to be gracious to me. Luke 15:4 says, "Suppose one of you had a hundred sheep and lost one. Wouldn't you leave the ninety-nine in the wilderness and go after the lost one until you found it?" God rejoices with all of the heavens when that lost sheep is found. Every prophet, Elijah, Moses, and Ezra, rejoices; every disciple, John, Matthew, Andrew, and Peter, rejoices. The angels, Jesus, and all your saved family rejoice for that lost sheep who came home, found by God. All of heaven rejoices when that lost sheep is found, repents, and is saved. I needed to be found, and all those guys I was with needed to be found too!

I wondered, *When will my Prince Charming come for his bride?* Did I only desire a loving dad, or was there more I was missing? I desired to be loved unconditionally, which I continued to think would be from a man.

I only wanted to date a true Christian man who would go to church and believe in God like me. I didn't even care about having kids of my own at this point, but I'd always wanted to foster children who felt abandoned and unloved. I wanted to love the children who weren't loved either, but discarded as nothing. I wondered, *Don't I need a husband to fulfill this dream, though?*

After Dan, I didn't date anyone for a while. I focused on finishing college, because I was almost done. I made a lot of friends in nursing school. Elenor was a friend I would help a lot in class. She was an amazing, hard-working woman who loved God. She was this tough Jamaican mom. She had a son named Keith. We used to carpool for clinicals in nursing school, which was so fun. We talked about everything all the time. I loved her.

So one day, we were talking about guys and wanting godly men, and I saw a picture of her son at school. I wanted to get my life together, and I wanted someone who wanted to get to know me for *me* and not what I could give him physically, or to look at me only physically. Elenor told him about me, and we exchanged numbers.

I didn't make a concrete decision in my mind to never fornicate again. All I knew was I wanted real love, and I knew that physical things got in the way of really getting to know someone. So I agreed to go on a date with him.

Keith decided to meet me for dinner at a mom-and-pop-style restaurant. He was romantic and older than me. I knew he would want commitment, and that's what I wanted at the time. Maybe that's why I didn't care about his age as much as I should have.

We had a great date. I was so nervous, giggling the whole time. The first thing I noticed about him was how he dressed. He wore bulky shoes, a tight shirt, and interesting jeans. He was bald when I met him, like my dad, but in the pictures he had hair.

I was already trying to settle my thoughts in my mind about the way he looked. He wasn't cute enough for me, but I was settling. He wasn't too open until he had a few drinks. I should've realized that was a red flag. He was also impatient, picky, and the way he portrayed himself made it seem like he grew up in the wrong crowd of people.

He was a very paranoid guy, like my dad in the way he would look around waiting for something to happen. He reminded me so much of my dad right away. I liked hanging out with him, but I wasn't set on him yet.

The night was coming to an end, and I finished my glass of wine just before we went to the back of the yard, a dark area near the restaurant where there was dancing and yard lights along the trees. I talk a lot when I'm nervous, so I kept talking. I knew he wanted to kiss me.

Then he pulled me in close to his belly, and he kissed me. I don't know how I felt about it, really. I think I liked it. We talked and kissed some more. Then we decided we should probably get home, because I drove like forty minutes to get there.

We were getting ready to leave. We were sitting in his car, then something happened that reminded me of the actions of all the guys I've experienced, and I instantly got sad. Instantly, all kinds of happiness went out the window. He grabbed my hand and I was devastated, but I told him no, I can't do that. I pretended that I was fine, but I wasn't. It felt like PTSD from everything I was trying to stay away from.

We said our goodbyes, and I called him on my ride home only because of the fear of falling asleep behind the wheel again after drinking some wine. I was afraid of that happening again, so I had to call him. I forgave him. He was sweet about it, so we talked more, and I felt safe again. I felt comfortable talking to him and enjoyed talking with him. I enjoyed talking to him the most out of all the guys I ever talked to. I felt like I could tell him anything.

I just cried writing that, because he really was a good guy, but without Jesus at the center of his life, he would never be the guy for me. And I wasn't the girl I wanted to be at that time either. I was so lost. Proverbs 21:2 says, "Every way of a man is right in his own eyes, but the LORD weighs the hearts."

We always think we are right or genuine at heart with our intentions, but the heart is deceitful. Most of the time we are deceiving ourselves, and the enemy is loving it, but God is grieved. God actually searches hearts for purity and true love. *Why do you want to talk to that attractive guy? Why are you willing to settle for this guy you really don't even find attractive?* Check your heart, check your ungodly intentions, and ask yourself the hard questions, the questions you fear to ask. Ask God to speak to you, and ask Him how much He loves you, please.

After that date, I started thinking about the distance right away. It reminded me of long-distance relationships like the one I had in the Dominican Republic. I thought nothing far away could stay close. That was how my brain worked. I compared every guy to a bad situation; there was always something similar about them that I hated. I wanted no more scars, and sometimes I wished I had no more memories.

As time passed, Keith would call me, and I would be busy, and wondering if I should pursue something that could hurt me. It was familiar and scary. I wasn't that into him, so we would catch up here and there, then suddenly he asked me out again. I said yes, because I wanted to go out for fun. Talking to him over the phone wasn't my preference for getting to know someone. I like face-to-face conversations the most.

Then, the morning of the date, I had another event to go to. I forgot all about him and forgot I'd already made plans to go to this birthday party on the same day of our date. He never reminded me and was upset, but he never told me he was angry. I found out months later how mad he was from that.

After that incident, he never asked me out again, so we stopped talking for about a month. One morning, I was driving Elenor to our clinical rotation at one of the well-known hospitals, and she started talking to her son on the phone and how he was now in school for his new license. I was very surprised to hear his voice. I used to like his voice a lot.

Once she got off the phone with him, she was telling me about their conversation and how there is this girl at church she was setting him up with, and he said, "At least Brielle has a shape and very nice hair." I was flattered back then, but now I'm grossed out to think I was flattered. I want a man to describe me not for my body but for my heart, and how I love God.

Because I was flattered about what he said, I began to wonder if he was still into me. So I ended up calling him that same night—with Elenor's permission, of course. He was very salty and annoyed that I'd left him hanging that day we had a date, and that I hadn't called or texted. I've always had the view that guys should make the first move to pursue a girl. He would make jokes about me being too busy to call him. I was laughing without realizing how he was already playing the victim way before we were even in a relationship.

We talked that night for a while after my clinical. He was the only guy I could talk about God to and he wouldn't get weird. I really appreciated that. We talked about life and God, and we joked. That was the start of really getting to know him, but I wish we'd just remained friends. We would have been better off as just friends, but then again, I wouldn't be who I am today without experiencing what I did with him.

We would talk every day more than I would talk to my best friend at this point. He worked and had class, and I had school, but we always found time to call to talk about everything under the sun. Emotional soul ties started to root and grow.

We went on a second date in Pennsylvania. I stayed over at his sister's house with her kids. We went to an Italian restaurant for our date. He had wine in his car—wine that I later spilled all over his car, wine that we were supposed to open at the restaurant. I was impressed with all the romance and effort. No guy would ever take me on dates and really plan something romantic.

Silly me tried to pop the wine bottle open, but it ended up bursting out everywhere. I was so embarrassed, but laughing. I think he was mad, but he kept his cool, and we tried to clean out his car. He told me later if I was anyone else he would have flipped out and thrown the person out. I should have known that was a red flag right away when he said that.

So we sat down at this cute restaurant and had calamari, spaghetti, and wine. I had so much food that I had to take some to go. Then he took me out bowling. I was so excited because I love playing games and sports. I lost in bowling somehow. Not my best sport.

We also played pool, which I was just OK at. He let me win, I think, even though I was teaching him how to hit the ball. I asked God if there was supposed to be something that comes out of this. Everyone wants a companion, a committed partner, and this guy happened to believe that Jesus is our Lord and Savior.

John 3:16 says, "For God so loved the world that He gave

His only begotten Son, that whoever believes in Him should not perish, but have everlasting life." He knew that believing in Him was better than not believing. John 3:18 says, "He who believes in Him is not condemned; but he who does not believe is condemned already, because he has not believed in the name of the only begotten Son of God." God sent Jesus to the world so that people might be saved through His blood.

I was confused about Keith, and I gave in to the confusion and let it lead our relationship instead of trusting my gut to walk away. I would always see the good in people. I let the relationship go with the flow without boundaries. No boundaries were made, but the Lord knows I wanted to make those boundaries. Where was my courage?

My courage wasn't found; no voice. I was so used to being silenced even though I always had so much to say. I wanted to have a godly relationship according to the Bible, a sinless relationship. 1 Corinthians 7: 1-2 says, "Yes it is good to abstain from sexual immorality, each man should have his own wife, and each woman should have her own husband."

The next date ruined me. I was so happy the first night after the first date because it was harmless, reserved; we were just getting to know each other. It was pure and real. I was true to myself, and I felt good about myself. There was no condemnation. The next date is when I already had a bad taste in my mouth.

He was supposed to pick me up after work from his sister's house, but he fell asleep. He finally woke up and picked me up late while I was already tired and tired of waiting. He came to pick me up, and I was staying at his place, or so I thought. We ended up getting food and going to a motel. He said he wanted to go to the club, but he overslept.

I was surprised, nervous, and upset, because he didn't warn me or tell me about something like this. If he'd told me, I would have told him I didn't want to stay in a hotel room with him. And his mom literally told me not to sleep with him. I know why she said that, because she must have known he would take me there. We ended up watching a movie at the hotel, which led to kissing and touching, but I had the strength to say no. It was the hardest thing ever, the temptation was heavy, because physical touch is my love language. It pains me to write my sins down now that I am free.

That night, I couldn't sleep at all. I was convicted, sexually aroused, disappointed, and actually afraid. For some reason, I was fearful of him, and I pretended to be sleeping because he was pacing up and down around the room. I was getting evil thoughts about him abusing me and wanting to kill me during the night. I was feeling a spirit of rape and murder and hate from him. I thought he was going to kill me, but I had no way out.

God must have warned me and protected me, because that spirit was very strong coming from him. I always could feel evil spirits ever since I was little. This was a warning from God that I should have listened to and run away. I thought to myself, *How did I let this happen?* He even told me that night when I said no to him that I was missing out. We clearly weren't on the same page about purity.

In the morning, when he was driving me, he was automatically more closed off, and the atmosphere was cold. I could feel spirits and discern the atmosphere of anger. It would have been the perfect time to tell him that we could never do that again, and that I wanted to wait until marriage to have sex; if he didn't agree with that, we wouldn't go out anymore. But I kept my mouth shut.

After this, I kept to myself. I didn't even want to tell Caity and Carrie. Eventually, like a week later, I did tell them. I told them how upset I was to be caught off-guard at a motel with him, and how I didn't want to hurt his feelings or seem ungrateful and rude. I was crying to them when I said that.

I also wasn't physically attracted to him. I felt close to him emotionally, intellectually, and spiritually aside from sexual sin. I never knew that when you live in sin, you could still think you know God, but you truly don't know God or how holy He is, and how He hates unholiness. When you live in sin, your whole life revolves around you and what you want and don't want. You never ask God what He wants from you.

I needed to be saved from myself. I always felt shameful, guilty, dirty, sad, and unworthy. Honestly, all of these things became true for me, like an unwanted identity. Proverbs 5:16 says, "Why spill the water of your springs in the streets, having sex with just anyone?" Isaiah 64:6 says, "We are all infected and impure with sin. When we display our righteous deeds; they are nothing, but filthy rags. Like autumn leaves, we wither and fall, and our sins sweep away like the wind."

I needed to open my heart to Jesus and truly let Him in. I needed resurrection and to be brought to life. John 11:25 says, "I am the resurrection and the life. Anyone who believes in me will live, even after dying." God loves us and wants us to surrender our lives to Him. To love and choose Him means to hate worldly things, worldly pleasure, speech, music, money, and addictions. Everything that keeps you away from God has to go.

Sex had to go for me—the fear, the shame, the guilt, the doubt, the sadness. These evil spirits brought more mental, physical, emotional, and spiritual baggage. I made soul ties with these guys, giving them pieces of my heart, body, and soul. I was no longer whole. I needed a Savior, Jesus, to break those soul ties. I needed deliverance from my own addictions and enslavements. I needed freedom from shackles, freedom from being a slave to fornication, to the desires of men.

Jesus, your teacher, savior, friend, first love, wants you to follow Him, and let Him take your heart to new depths—depths of an abundant life. He wants to replace your burdens with His, because His are easy and light. He wants to speak to your heart tenderly in the wilderness, so it's just you and Him left to get to know each other at your truest form. In the wilderness with God is the way to know whose you are, who you'll be, and how much you are truly loved. No one loves you the way Jesus loves you, I promise you that.

Chapter Ten

WHERE IS MY PRINCE CHARMING?

I didn't realize it then—and honestly, if I had known it then, I probably wouldn't have accepted it yet. All I knew for the years 2017 through 2020 was sadness, pain, trauma, uselessness, tears, unworthiness, lovelessness, and shame. I couldn't understand where this emptiness came from; it just stayed in me for years, which led to more and more sinful shame.

I lost my soul with the trauma first and then the sin. Little did I know that behind the scenes, my Father in heaven had been running toward me with a plan to save me the whole time. The whole time I put myself in a deeper, darker hole. And I thank God that I didn't die young in my sin, because I would have been sent to hell right away.

I believed in God, as many people say. I believed Jesus died for me, but I didn't know the love of what that meant and the purity and the relationship in his sacrifice. I thought I was saved and baptized, but I was a sinner going into the water like taking a bath, without changing. I was still just a sinner coming out of the dirty water.

I was fooling myself, deceived by Satan. I would have lived in everlasting torment, in hell, if I didn't give my heart to Jesus, if I didn't choose Him instead of my sin, and if I didn't surrender my whole life to Him completely, especially the pain of my broken family and broken relationships with my dad and many men. Fornication and resentment was my middle name.

———

Keith came just toward the end of my sinful journey. Please feel conviction if you are reading this. If you are feeling convicted, know this: God only convicts you; no human can. God convicts the ones he loves, and guess what? That's you.

Hebrews 12:1-2 says, "Therefore, since we are surrounded by such a huge crowd of witnesses to the life of faith, let us strip off every weight that slows us down, especially the sin that so easily trips us up, and let us run with endurance the race God has set before us. We do this by keeping our eyes on Jesus, the author and finisher of our faith. Because of the joy awaiting him, he endured the cross, despising the shame. Now he is seated in the place of honor beside God's throne."

The Bible also says in Hebrews 12:4–5, "After all, you have not yet given your lives in your struggle against sin." And have you forgotten the encouraging words God spoke to you as His children? He said, "My child, don't make light of the Lord's discipline, and don't give up when he corrects you, for the Lord disciplines those He loves, and He punishes each one He accepts as His child."

I needed to give my life in my struggle against sin. If I was being disciplined, it would mean I was a loved child of God. I wanted to be loved—who doesn't? I was so blinded by the great conversations Keith and I had over the phone that I didn't notice they were never the same when we were in person. I never understood that.

Biblically, faith has to do with the things you cannot see, but the things you hear about Christ. Whenever I got to see Keith, that wonder and awe would fade away. Then, instead of talking, we would just use physical intimacy to make up for the lack of connection that I wanted to feel. I was unsatisfied once again. God's love never fades away, though. It was God's love I always needed, not a selfish man's lust.

I talked to Keith on the phone almost every day after that. I told him I wanted to wait until marriage, and he said he wanted to as well, but that wasn't realistic for him because he had never done it. He didn't want to change or try—a red flag that should have led me to run away, but I didn't take what he said as a definite. I thought maybe, for me, he would change his mind.

I wanted to stick to my gut, but I was so timid and easily manipulated. I remember the disappointment in my heart that day. I felt like a child crying inside, just asking him, "But why? The Bible says it's sin. Why?" The worst part is, I stayed. I didn't run away.

Never go into a relationship hoping someone will do something out of their nature or own strength for you. Our strength to do things or to change always fails. People don't change unless God Himself changes their heart and that person willingly wants to change. Do not date someone for who you want them to be. Take them as they are, or leave them alone.

God took me in as I was and spoke to my heart when I was done living by my own standards, at a time when I didn't want to have all control over everything, a time when I let myself be vulnerable enough, and honest with my own heart. My heart wasn't just broken, it was also very tired. I had a tired spirit, tired of hurting others, tired of letting people hurt me, tired of feeling so stuck, and tired of making the wrong choices.

I wanted my life to really matter, to have a life that touched people's hearts, a life that would bring heaven to earth every day. I wanted to stop living for myself and start living for others, for something bigger than myself. I always had a serving heart, and

I always thought my kindness was a weakness, because people would always take advantage of me. Now I am thankful for the heart I have, and I wouldn't give it up for anything.

I thought Keith would protect my heart, but my heart was never his to protect. I was fooled by the outer appearance of a protective, strong persona. We have to surrender our hearts to God, to our first love; only then we will know how to guard our hearts as the Lord says to.

I truly believe Keith loved me in a way he thought was love. The issue was, we didn't love God like we thought we did, nor ourselves enough. We could've never loved each other the way God intended. God was there always, but our surrender wasn't. We were living in sin, slaves to fornication, slaves to fear.

At one point, I was so afraid of pregnancy that I started to use contraception to have control. I didn't want my own kids. I wanted to foster, then hopefully adopt someday. Keith told me about his experience with a foster kid in his home, trying to talk me out of it. I was certain that I wanted to do that. He didn't like the idea, but he didn't leave me knowing that. I wonder why he didn't.

After the IUD, I never felt the same body-wise. I gained so much weight without even trying, and I always felt gross, unclean. He knew about the discomfort and was angry about it, because my pain would disrupt things and what he wanted. Most of the time, I would be afraid of the pain and would restrain from fornication, which he was also very angry about.

As with every relationship I ever had, we began to talk less and less about our hearts and real things like the Bible, and being honest about what was going on with ourselves. I barely talked about my family issues, but I always talked about all the guys I used to talk to because he would talk about girls from his past very little. He was very secretive, and I was jealous.

He was very uncomfortable sharing his emotions and secrets. I hated when he didn't want to share. I was sharing my body, but he couldn't even share his thoughts or his heart. I held a lot of things in because that is what I was used to doing. It was a learned, defeating habit.

Brielle, brush it off, keep moving forward, you are fine. This is killing you, but you are going to be OK, I kept telling myself. But I wasn't OK, and I wasn't going to be OK. There were so many times when we were going on dates, but unofficially, he would shut me out. He told me how he wanted to keep his options open, and he wouldn't answer when I asked him if he was going on dates with other people or talking to other girls.

I realize now that all of that was a game, a way to keep control. The secrets actually pulled me closer to him, because now it seemed like a challenge for me. I was definitely falling back into something I was familiar with, like a dog returning to its own vomit. As the Bible says in 2 Peter 2:22, "A washed pig returns to the mud."

Foolish! It took me crying about being hurt, and telling him I loved him, to just be officially dating. I was being manipulated to receive commitment. This happened months after talking, and on a getaway date that I was so excited about but turned into something only pleasing for him, only pleasing for his own desires. I felt like I was too far gone to say no, and I wanted to please him too. My soul was dying.

As I am writing this, I feel everything as if I am back in it, as if I wasn't redeemed and saved from it all. My wounds left a mark, and my heart is heavy. I am so sorry to every girl who did everything to please a guy but came out of it with a shattered heart and a lost soul. I see you and I know you with all my heart. I am sorry that you didn't love yourself enough and God enough to speak up for yourself. I'm sorry you weren't courageous enough to leave sooner. I'm sorry you didn't think you could heal. I am so sorry you thought there was no way out, but I am here to tell you there is a way out, and the way has a name: Jesus.

Abba! Jesus is your savior. Jesus is the living water you have
been so thirsty for, lost girl. Jesus is your one, your one and only,
true first love. "The woman said to Jesus, 'Sir, you have nothing to
draw with, and the well is deep. Where then do you get that living
water?'" (John 4:11). Jesus answered and said to her, "Whoever
drinks of this water will thirst again, but whoever drinks of the
water that I shall give him will become in him a fountain of water
springing up into everlasting life" (John 4:14).

Asking Jesus to save you, and giving him your whole life, is
the greatest choice you will ever make. Not only will you never be
thirsty for life and love ever again, but you'll have everlasting life
with the One who saved you, Jesus, the only one who loves you
like no one else possibly could. Jesus will be the peace you breath
in every day, and the love you capture every day, and the joy you
bring every day. Jesus will be your everything—that's a promise!
You'll desire to live for him, die for him even. I am a fountain of
water springing up in everlasting life thanks to Jesus, my God, my
Father, my First Love, my Husband.

I hope whoever is reading this has figured out by now that this
isn't a story just about some girl's testimony. This is a love story to
you from Jesus, your Lord and Savior! It is not a coincidence that
you are reading this. This is ordained for you to read. God chose
you. He loves you!

The Holy Spirit has led me and anointed my hands to write
this love story to you—a love story to draw you close to God, to
tell you He doesn't care about what you have done, all He wants is
you to come running into His open arms. He wants you to know
that everything you ever wanted and needed is in Him. He wants
to heal your heart and have all of you. He knows you more than
you know yourself. Life will make sense, and you'll know who
you belong to.

Take a chance, one chance. Give God one chance. He is the
one person who will never forsake you. He is the one person who
will never let you down. The Author and Finisher of your faith

sees you and knows your heart. His thoughts for you are vast. "Mightier than the waves of the sea is this love for you" (Psalms 93:4). "More than the grains of sand are His thoughts towards you" (Psalms 139:18).

Will you take a leap of faith and give Jesus a chance? God loves you. He loves Keith. He loves all people. I pray that you and Keith get to know Jesus the way I do now. What a privilege it is to know God.

Satan attempted to destroy two people who wanted the truth and love but were searching in the wrong places. Satan will never win because he has already been defeated by God Almighty Himself. Jesus defeated death and killed sin on the cross so that we could know God and have a relationship with Him forever.

—✦—

Keith's and my story was broken because we were already broken people in need of a savior. We continued to be together in codependency, leading me to become more and more upset all the time. I felt like I was going insane. The more verbal tension, the more emotional manipulation, the more I stayed.

There was one experience that really threw me over the edge. I told him I was going to a friend's house from my old university for her sister's birthday. I told him it was a family party because it was. They were Christians too, though lukewarm ones.

The moment I got there and started catching up on life with my friends, I sent him a picture of me eating and with everyone in the background. Keith saw guys in the background and began to get possessive. He told me to leave without letting me speak or explain that these were just her family members. This had nothing to do with me. I told him I didn't know them and I was there for my friends. I remember trying to explain myself to him as if I was doing something wrong.

Then it got worse. I told him I just got there and it took like forty minutes to drive there. Plus, it would be embarrassing to leave.

He began to ask me what I was wearing, if I was going in the pool there, and if I was talking to guys there. I told him I was wearing shorts and a long T-shirt, like I usually wear in the summer. He begins to say things like, "Oh, so you are wearing booty shorts for guys to look at you and to get attention from all the guys, and I bet you are going in the pool because you are wearing a bathing suit." He continued to belittle me and my character.

Then he gave me an ultimatum that killed my heart, threatening me if I didn't leave the party. He said, "If you don't leave, I guess we will have to be in an open relationship. You can do what you want with the guys there, and I will do whatever I want with other girls." I was speechless and crying, feeling as if I was in a nightmare.

I ended up leaving the party, numb like I used to feel for years before. I called him back while I was driving and told him I left, because he told me to call him when I left. He sounded relieved, but I could barely speak. I could barely feel. I was dead inside, so confused, and I knew this couldn't be love. He was talking to me on the phone, and I was not present at all. I was in shock, and I shut down.

He was saying that I sounded like I wanted to break up with him, because at this point I told him I needed a break from him. I had stopped feeling anything. So I told him I needed a break, and he started asking me for how long, and I said like a week or so to think and to see what I was feeling. It became a battle to just get him to understand that I didn't want to talk to him for at least a week, and he didn't even do that. After only three days, he texted me this Kirk Franklin song that made him think of me. Honestly, I was disgusted by him and the way he was acting.

During this time, I kept busy. COVID-19 was still closing schools and churches. I spent most of my days at Carrie's house, so sad and numb. I was the health care coordinator for the summer camp and day care I worked at for years, my favorite job in the world, while I was going through this with Keith. I also was blessed to remain in nursing school while working there. I did online classes and worked at my favorite place while spending time with Caity and Carrie.

It was perfect for me to be with children because they always had a way of loving me and making me smile and feel free. Children brought me hope. I had many moments at the camp when I would just break down crying, having flashbacks, PTSD, of the moments that broke my heart. Being with Keith opened back up past hurts from before him as well—lies of the enemy about myself and my worth. I was actually going through this trauma when I hadn't fully healed from the first trauma. I had so much baggage, and I ended up adding to it.

A few people caught me upset, crying, or staring into space. I told the ones who noticed: Alexa, Chris, and Trisha. Alexis understood completely because she has been so strong when she went through all the same things as me. Trisha had just broken up with an overprotective boyfriend. When I was telling Chris what happened, I instantly realized I couldn't tell Keith that I talked to another guy about him, and instantly I cried again because this was my reality.

Chris told me that he used to be angry all the time and that it's something the man has to work through on his own, and how I didn't deserve to be treated that way. I hoped I would never be treated that way again, and I feared it. Honestly, it's a fear I have to continue to declare God's truth over that there is no fear in love, and we were made without fear. Fear is from the enemy.

———

A little more than a week passed, and I was forgiving Keith, but I was still very much hurting. I needed more time, but he didn't want to let me go, and I didn't want to hurt his feelings. I didn't want to give up on him, and he said he had changed and God had been working on him. He talked about how his anger was built up from stress from working on the road as a truck driver all the time, and that he needed something more consistent and steady.

I didn't believe him at all, nor did I trust him, but I still gave him a second chance. I told him that if this happened again, I was done. After that, it was OK for maybe a month—and then he picked me up and met my dad, which was very weird. I could tell my dad didn't vibe with him. It was almost like they were testing each other, but then there was a handshake.

I wondered if my dad would say anything about him. Deep down, I wanted my dad to tell me he didn't like Keith and that I deserved better, because I think deep down I knew I did. I needed someone to intervene and tell me I was making a huge mistake for taking him back.

But no one knew all he did, so how could anyone save me, especially my dad, who had already shattered my heart? Later on, after Keith picked me up, we went to my friend's party. Once we got to the party, he started drinking. I'd asked him not to drink around me, because it gets very bad when he drinks. He is a thousand times worse when he is drunk.

Oscar was at the party—an old friend I hadn't seen since high school, and everyone who knows me knows that I love everyone and am very open about it. That day, Oscar took pictures of Keith and me, but I didn't realize Keith was so jealous and mad at me for saying something to Oscar. We were talking to Oscar about his photography and seeing if maybe he could take photos of us. I was so intrigued and proud of Oscar and all of his creative work.

We were standing next to my friend's pool. Keith was next to me. I was so excited for Oscar and his future endeavors, so out of joy and love, I said, "Wow, I love you and all you're doing for people through your art and photography. That's truly amazing when you are doing it for the community." I didn't even realize Keith's anger and jealousy when he heard me say that. Apparently,

I messed up big time in front of Keith. But it was so natural for me to encourage Oscar.

I remember after we took pictures with Oscar, Keith got quiet and distant. He began to drink a lot, and I started to see he was getting more aggressive and drunk. I tried to tell him to stop drinking, but he wouldn't listen.

The night got worse. I should have gone home or asked my family for a ride home, but I didn't—maybe because I was embarrassed. Keith and I slept over that night, and Keith didn't speak to me. Instead, he had his way with my body to get a sense of control again. I knew he was trying to prove a point.

In the morning, I felt so defiled, as if I was just his object to use and discard whenever he wanted. I continued to bring up why he drank so much last night. I had been tipsy but not drunk. I forced him to tell me what was happening with him. He used me that night for pleasure when he was actually mad at me and jealous of Oscar.

He said, "You should be with Oscar instead of me because you love him so much. You were giving him googly eyes, and you don't look at me like that."

In my mind, I was enraged. I couldn't believe he couldn't just talk to me, but instead he wanted to be a child and throw tantrums. That was why I broke up with him in the first place. I thought, *How is he thirty and thinking and acting like this?* Yeah, my life was a ridiculous movie I didn't want to be featured in.

I was devastated once again. We were fighting this time around. I was so done with him and the garbage he pulled with the secrets. I was yelling on the phone that whole night. He kept saying, "This isn't the sweet Brielle I know, the loving Brielle." I thought, *No, this wasn't the quiet Brielle, taking maltreatment anymore. I can't just allow this without fighting for myself.*

I really wanted to break up with him. He kept playing the victim and saying, "You're not loving me by raising your voice, so everything you said about loving me must have been a lie." I'd had it. I got like four hours of sleep that night trying to figure out how to end this relationship. Why did I give him a second chance? He hadn't changed.

The same night, I talked to Mel, and she told me everything Keith told her boyfriend the night of the party. I felt so sick as Mel told me to end it. In and out of sleep through the night, I woke up before my nursing clinical rotation with a text from my mom saying, "Don't let anyone dim your light." She must have heard me yelling at him and crying all through the night. My mom had to hear that. It broke my heart that she had to hear all that.

I can take pain, but the moment someone I love so much who loves me so much has to feel my pain, I can't do it. I never want to be a burden, because people leave burdens, people give up on love, people give up on people, people give up on me. That is why I never told my mom what was happening. I do wonder what would've happened if I did tell my mom. Maybe speaking the truth would've saved me a lot of heartbreak and trauma.

I had no tears left in me for days. I felt so ashamed, like the most naive girl in the world. I wanted to blame all of this on my dad, but I wonder if I blamed God too. If my dad had never filled our hearts with deceit, maybe I would have more respect for myself, maybe I would see myself as beautiful and worthy of love—love that would stay and never threaten to leave.

I wondered what it would be like to receive love without giving up my body. Was it possible? Could I be loved unconditionally? I didn't want to live a life of lies filled with liars. How could I let myself be treated like this a second time?

I think I couldn't talk to my mom because for so long, I'd been taking care of her, trying to keep the peace, and trying to protect her frailty of heart, but in reality, I was useless, incapable, and out of control. Everything with Dad kept me from sharing my pain. I didn't want her to carry this pain I was carrying on top of her own. I just needed to stay strong. *Brielle you can't crumble. Be strong. Don't cry.* Suppression kills, but we'd both already had too much to bear. I wish I'd told her, but I was scared she would break.

In reality, though, God used Mom to save me through that text message that day. Moms love us, and they want us to know. Even though she was heartbroken, she still had the capacity to love me and fight for me. I thanked my mom for saving my life, being my angel from God all my life. She was the clarity I needed, my way out. "No temptation has overtaken you except such as is common to man; but God is faithful, who will not allow you to be tempted beyond what you are able, but with the temptation will also make the way of escape, that you may be able to bear it" (1 Corinthians 10:13).

Mom knows me for who I am, a joyful person even when I'm not happy or OK. God spoke through my mom to give me courage to do what I was meant to do for a while now. So I called Keith right away, without much sleep, and before my online clinical rotation at seven o'clock. I told him, "I can't do this anymore," sounding very dead on the phone. "We are just very different, and we want different things in a relationship. I don't fit your standards, and I'm not going to change who I am."

He basically said OK and hung up the phone. He was beyond prideful. I knew he was very hurt. He called back after that a few times, but I had no energy to answer, and I wasn't going to because I had nothing else to say. I was at my weakest, yet my strongest to say what I should have said a long time ago. By the grace of God, by His strength alone, I survived.

—∞—

Keith continued to text and call me. I ignored everything. Because I didn't answer my phone, he began to Snapchat me and shove God in my face. He started to say things like, "God wouldn't like the way you are ignoring me and treating me this way as if I cheated on you or something." He would try to spiritually manipulate me. He kept texting aggressively, thinking he didn't deserve all these boundaries.

Elenor, his mom, told me he was very sad, but I was sad too and beaten up mentally and emotionally. I felt free just from not speaking to him. I was in double bondage with him, and I thank God I was set free.

I didn't talk to him until a year later, and that was because I accidentally picked up the phone as a random number popped up. I had no idea it was him. My heart sank to my stomach.

He didn't call to apologize. He called on September 19, 2021, telling me about how he was near my house and wondered if I still looked the same and lived in the same place, and how I was. He asked if I still had Brielle hair and to not be a stranger. No apology, nothing. He still thought he did nothing wrong.

In my head, I thought, *I definitely will be a stranger.* I prayed that he wouldn't come after me or come to my house. I was being very vague on the phone and just let him speak. I was so upset that I was speaking to him, but I still needed healing from him.

Everything disgusted me: his voice, his pride, his ignorance, and how I felt toward him. I do have hope that God will capture his heart someday. God is hope. I have forgiven him many times, and I continue to still. God says to forgive people seventy times seven times. I continue to bless him, though our soul ties were broken.

God never meant for us to give our heart away to many people or for it to be broken constantly. I felt so free from him, but sometimes I would get nervous with thoughts that he would just show up at my house one day. I still wondered if I would ever truly be healed from all this: first my dad and then all the men, and all the trauma that lingered.

If I was still with Keith, I definitely believe I could have been dead, or our relationship would have been irreversibly destructive to me mentally and emotionally. Words fall short of how thankful I am to God for giving me the strength to end that relationship. Now I must rest. "I will both lie down in peace and sleep for You alone, O LORD make me dwell in safety" (Psalm 4:8).

Healing and to be healed is what we all want for ourselves, for our loved ones, for our friends, and even for our enemies, isn't it? How can I love someone if I am not healed myself, if I don't love myself? I wish I could say that right after breaking up with Keith, I gave my life to Christ and God saved me right away. That wasn't my story yet. But God was revealing to me a lot of hurt and pain that was still deep rooted in me.

After that breakup, I was still empty, but I knew it was the right choice. I started trying to have fun again, going out, drinking with coworkers, with old friends from college, doing things I had stopped doing for a while. With these things, I felt good for a moment, so good and so happy. I wished I could feel that free and happy all the time, but I knew I never would, because every time I did this stuff I felt more empty, needy, unloved, and lonely eventually—every time I was alone or the buzz wore off.

I felt like this cycle was never-ending. I was talking to this guy I called K on Snapchat, just for attention. I spoke to him because I was like, *Why not?*, but I shouldn't have because I needed healing. So I tried to fill my void once again. When would I learn? I went to any and every party I was invited to. Then I met a guy I called Z at two parties with my college friends.

A lot of my friends lived double lives when it came to faith. I only knew lukewarm Christians who lived in sin Monday through Saturday but showed up at church on Sunday. Carrie, Caity, and my mom were the only true examples of people who believed in Jesus and proved that truth by the way they lived. I hadn't truly surrendered to God yet, but I knew I didn't want to die and go to hell. I was a lukewarm Christian claiming I knew God but not living a righteous life to prove that I knew God.

I noticed that lukewarm Christians would party, drink, never talk about God, fornicate, curse, and watch and listen to worldly music and movies while committing sin and believing they would be in heaven someday. I knew I was going to hell, but it seemed as though lukewarm Christians thought they could abuse God's grace by living for Satan but claiming to know God. Demons know God too; demons know Scripture too; they believe too. So I knew I was a hypocrite. I realized where I was going. Matthew 7:21–23 says:

> Not everyone who says to Me, "Lord, Lord," shall enter the kingdom of heaven, but he who does the will of My Father in heaven. Many will say to Me on that day, "Lord, Lord, have we not prophesied in Your name, cast out demons in Your name, and done many wonders in Your name?" And then I will declare to them, "I never knew you; depart from Me, you who practice lawlessness!"

God speaks about lukewarm Christians in Revelation 3:16: "but since you are like lukewarm water, neither hot nor cold, I will spit you out of my mouth!" God would spit me out if I continued on this path; I knew it. God gives us the choice between life or death, hot or cold, God or Satan, to be slaves to sin or slaves to righteousness, to practice sin or to flee from it. We can't serve two masters.

I wondered for a long time why I felt so alone. It was because I truly served Satan, not God. Because of my actions, the way I was living represented Satan. Deuteronomy 30:19 says:

> Today I have given you the choice between life and death, between blessings and curses. Now I call on heaven and earth to witness the choice you make. Oh, that you would choose life so that you and your descendants might live!

I desired to live. I wanted to make a good choice. I desired for my descendants to live. How could I truly live? Would God even love someone like me? Would God leave me, abandon me, lie to me and my family like my earthly dad did? Carrie and Caity call Him Father and Friend. What kind of Father and Friend would He be for me? Could I be His, or would He reject me too?

I wanted to know about Jesus, but I had no idea where to start. I said the salvation prayer with my mouth every time I went to church, but nothing happened. All I knew was this life of sin and flings. After falling right back into sin with Z, I was disappointed, upset again with feelings I was so familiar with. These choices I continued to make kept me bound.

I wanted to feel wanted, to feel seen. Z was a sweet gentleman, and we seemed to get along and be super-flirty. It seemed harmless for a little while, but once again I fell. I gave into temptation once again.

I remember talking to Caity about it, trying to hide my shame by telling myself, *It's OK, I didn't let it get too far.* Caity knew I was better than that, so much better than that, but she never let me be ashamed, even though I already felt so inadequate to change. After confessing all of it to her, I texted him, and we talked for a little bit. I wanted to be normal and have a real relationship, but I wasn't ready, so I spoke to Z about just taking it slow and getting to know each other. We both talked about how we recently got out of relationships and agreed to just be friends.

Then we decided to go out on a dinner date. He drove about forty minutes to come pick me up from my house. He took me out to this restaurant near my house with yummy wings. I was so nervous. I still weirdly felt numb, though, like I was without feelings. My soul had been downcast for so long.

We sat at the table together, and I was the only one keeping conversation going. He was so closed off, but not in a nervous way. I even felt like I was boring him. I started to laugh nervously when I would ask him questions about his life. He gave me very vague answers. I felt super insecure and so out of place, so bewildered, because I was so talkative and he wasn't. The attraction was there, but I knew he had a lot of pain in his heart.

I wanted to help him, but I knew there was nothing I could do. People have so much pain in their hearts, you can just feel it, the presence of pain and sorrow. Everyone hides their pain, but I see it more than anything now, and feel it instantly, so much so that there is no point of hiding it. Hidden things are never noticed, never changing, never growing. God knows all things, and He wants to bring all that darkness to the light so it loses its power. Mark 4:22 says, "For nothing is hidden except to be revealed; nor has anything been secret, but that it would come to light."

Z couldn't even put on a fake smile. I could tell his soul was far away, lost, on a quest to find himself. I could relate to his heart's cry. I could almost tangibly feel it through him. Does God hear our heart's tantrum to be saved? Why would He let all this happen to my mom and our family? Did he even care?

I think that is what God tries to tell us, but we are too afraid to let Him into our hearts, even though He already knows it all. He was there when all the pain entered into our hearts, but I just couldn't feel Him, as if there was a shield keeping me away from understanding. He must have seen my dad in the act of adultery. He must have seen my mom fainting. He must have seen my brother's silent tears. He must have seen me breaking like shattered glass, dying to feel again, yet scared to.

I was at the edge of the cliff knowing one touch could truly destroy me. He must have known and allowed it all. An all-powerful God allows all this pain, but He has to have a plan through it all. Doesn't he have a plan for me?

Oh Lord, You have searched me and known me. You know my sitting down and my rising up; You understand my thoughts afar off. You comprehend my path and my lying down, and are acquainted with all my ways. For there is not a word on my tongue, but behold, O Lord, You know it altogether.
—Psalms 139:1–4

Chapter Eleven

NOW FOUND

Z drove me home after dinner, and we shared a kiss goodnight. Even though I didn't want to go on another date with him, I liked how there was a quick kiss goodnight and that was all, that was it, nothing more. I went inside loving the sense of purity reached, of hope.

I sobbed so much that night. I didn't believe that was possible. It was the feeling of innocence that I wished I'd had the very first time I really liked a boy—the innocence I had before Dad broke my confidence, safety, and hope in men. I craved purity and innocence so much. I craved true love and protection and deep kindness. I craved a friendship filled with purity, honesty, and love that would become a committed relationship at the altar.

I wanted to start over and learn how to love again as a young virgin girl, pure and filled with joy. Starting over began to seem possible for the first time. Maybe God really did have a plan for me after all.

———

It was September 11 when Carrie and I were celebrating Caity's twenty-fifth birthday at her house because the two of them were going to church for Friday night service. I was wondering why I wasn't invited. They asked me if I wanted to go, but I was dressed in tight jeans and a cropped shirt, so I knew I wasn't dressed appropriately.

I decided to stay at Caity's house to help her mom with a Webex link for her chemistry class. I spent some quality time with their mom. I told Caity I would go the following Friday. Little did I know my whole life was about to change. I was about to change forever.

After I was finished helping Caity's mom, I went home to read the book I had borrowed from Caity: *Relationship Goals* by Michael Todd. I got home after a lonely, teary-eyed drive. This was common for me after coming home from their house. I always came home to a life I didn't like or ever imagine for myself.

I showered and went to read on my couch next to my window. No one was home, and I was so sad reading. I was thinking about all I had done and how I didn't want to live anymore. The edge of that cliff seemed very close, very real. What was I living for?

I was reading a small footnote of scripture in the book when I felt a strong gentle presence wash over me. My eyes were opened as I began to see myself. I saw myself as if my life was flashing before me from an old film camera.

Three-dimensional films of my life were set up in boxes of time. I saw me and my ex in a room. I saw myself crying myself to sleep. I saw myself ashamed of my sin and not knowing if I could go on. I saw myself in agony. But all the films had one thing in common: Jesus. In the doorway, there was Jesus looking at me with loving eyes filled with tears. Our tears matched.

I felt like I was there for so long in this experience. I wanted to stay forever outside of my body. I finally understood how Jesus sees me. I am His everything. You are His everything. When I cried, He cried. When I suffered, He suffered. When I didn't believe, He was so sad that I didn't believe.

In the speed of light, I knew I'd been loved all this time.

Instantly, I knew I had an unconditional loving Father who saw me. I was known by Jesus. He was always there, especially when I thought I was so alone, when I hated myself, when I thought I could never be cherished or safe. Jesus was in the doorway. He was always knocking at the door of my heart. He was those fragments of joy I held on to. He was the one who sent Caity and Carrie, my angels. He was the Father I yearned for, the one I wanted to dance with. He found my lost heart.

I fell to my knees in repentance, crying out, "Jesus, I'm so sorry. I didn't know. I'm so sorry you had to see me like this, and you were intensely understanding everything I've ever felt. I'm so sorry I caused you so much pain. Forgive me. I don't want to live this way anymore. Take my life. I need You."

I sobbed for what seemed like twenty minutes. His presence was so tangible, and I felt so light. Every burden was lifted off. I could truly breathe. I was finally at peace. I was dead, and now I'm alive.

My dad could have never filled that aching in me, because my dad was never my rescuer. Jesus always was! I'm His, and He chose my dad to raise me. My whole life, I've had a good heavenly Father right next to me. It was always Jesus who consoled me. His Spirit, the Comforter, did it all. He comforted "those who mourn in Zion, to give them beauty for ashes, the oil of joy for mourning, the garment of praise for the spirit of heaviness; that they may be called trees of righteousness, the planting of the LORD, that He may be glorified" (Isaiah 61:3 NKJV).

He gave me beauty from death, anointed me with joy for my grief, and placed His blanket of praise over me so the spirit of heaviness would leave. Now I am on a firm foundation, rooted in my Abba's hands. The Father I never thought I had loved me exceedingly. He removed that deep sorrow from my lost heart.

In seconds, Jesus changed my mind and heart. I was so worth it that He didn't only meet me on my couch, but He took my death on the cross more than two thousand years ago. So sweet the sound of His voice is; I pray you hear Him too. He has taken me away with Him in His heart, a love that flows beyond all I can imagine. For Jesus, I am enough. All at once, He opened my eyes, mind, and heart to know Him.

I saw another miracle that same night and the next morning. He took all the boys off my phone that very night. One blocked me, and the other disappeared and stopped texting me completely. I was free beyond measure, and I no longer contemplated my purpose anymore, because He was my reason to live.

I was no longer bound to fornication and all types of sin. I hated sin, and I knew I was forgiven. I knew one day I would be walking home into heaven with Jesus by my side for eternity. I wasn't scared anymore; protection filled my every void. This time, I would walk through life hand in hand with my Creator, as I was made to do. My heavenly Father was the one I needed all along. He never left me. I was never alone, never judged, and always wanted!

My heart filled with forgiveness, and the desire for reconciliation with my dad was heavy and prominent. All the hate and disappointment was gone toward my dad. I had this new sense of love, mercy, and compassion toward him. My dad was truly forgiven, and so was my past. I was made new and so happy.

I told everyone I knew about Jesus and what He did for me. Some friends stayed, others blocked me, but I wasn't worried. I wanted everyone I knew and loved to know that I had been going to hell before Jesus saved me. I told people how I accepted Him into my heart and turned away from sin. I wanted to share Him because I knew He truly loved all His children and wanted them to be saved, so not one would perish.

My God has this great, great love for my dad that I felt on the inside of my soul. I prayed for my dad's heart and his salvation every day after the night I experienced God. Jesus's heart is the most pure, genuine, just, and sacrificial. This was the man who died for us all on the cross—the death I deserved, but He took my place and my dad's place because He said we were worth it. He said, "Father, forgive them for they do not know what they are doing" (Luke 23:34).

I cried for so long thinking about Jesus's tears for me over the years. The vision playing over in my spirit watching how Jesus saw me not believe in Him, and seeing the lack of love I had for myself. I hated that I was so brutally against my dad for so long, because Jesus loves him so much. Only God knows my father's heart and why he did all he did.

I repented every day, as my heart continued to change and become more compassionate. For years, I had cheated on the only man who truly loved me. I was Gomer in the book of Hosea.

I told God that evening, "I want to know You and I want to live for You. I can't do this anymore, I am so sorry, please take my life, forgive me, and change me. God, I know these guys I am talking to are from me, my control. I don't want control anymore. My way is wrong and painful, and I can't live with this resentment anymore. I surrender to you, Lord. Please take these guys out of my life."

The next morning, I experienced more of God's peace, love, and joy like never before. Surrender is beautiful. God "desires mercy and not sacrifice." He wants our love and a relationship with Him. He wants us to know Him.

Hosea is the husband of an adulterous wife, Gomer. It is my story with God, and my parents' story. I was addicted to sin, loving my sin more than my God. Just like my dad, I've been sinful, an adulterer. Over and over again, I turned my back on God, but Jesus never gave up on me, nor did He forsake me. He had many mercies toward me and my dad.

He spoke to my heart while I was at my worst. Hosea 2:14 says, "I will allure her, I will bring her into the wilderness, And speak comfort to her." And in verse 16: "that you will call Me my Husband, and no longer call Me my Master." He took away all of the men I talked to and wanted to talk to almost like an invisible cloak of armor. Guys would reach out, but God's cloak deflected them from my interest.

Since the day I surrendered and every day since, I have the title and heart of a bride, God's betrothed. "I will betroth you to Me forever; yes, I will betroth you to Me in righteousness and justice, In lovingkindness and mercy; I will betroth you to Me in faithfulness, and you shall know the LORD'" (Hosea 2:19–20). This is God's perfect promise for you and me!

You are perfect and more than worthy. You are betrothed. Jesus is our Prince Charming. We will always be daddy's little girls, both on this side of heaven and for our eternity with Jesus. No matter what our dads have done here in this broken world, Jesus will always be enough for us. Nothing can separate us from His love. It's infinite.

Dear God,

You relentlessly loved me when I was in sexual sin, when I didn't know You, and when I despised my own dad. You spoke to me tenderly when men hurt me my whole life with their words, actions, selfishness, pride, and addictions. You spoke to my broken heart in the wilderness, and I knew I was found by You! You took me home into Your arms and, for the first time in my life, I felt so safe. I could breathe again without pain, without waiting for the next crisis to break me again. You saved me, and I began to smile again and danced with You in my kitchen. That sweet little girl came back to life more beautiful than before. I was made by the King of Kings who never left me. The One King who desired

ONCE LOST NOW FOUND

*me and made me worthy of abounding love, and
to be loved fully!*

*Love Yours,
Brielle*

———

I've learned about a loving Father who cherishes His daughters. I've learned about a perfect Father who changed my heart completely. He loosed chains as I let go of all anger and resentment toward my dad. I love him so much, and I've forgiven him with all my heart. We laugh again and joke. I give him forehead kisses, and I squeeze him tight. I correct him and respect him. I pray for his salvation, and there's so much hope for him.

I praise God for healing and the opportunity to cry out and write this love story to not just you all but also to my dad and many who have experienced the pain of *once lost, now found*. I see my dad's flaws and scars, and I love him more for them because when I see his scars, it reminds me of Jesus being pierced with the torture we all deserved on the cross. Jesus didn't just die for my sin but for my daddy's sins too.

I trusted God, and He didn't only save me but He saved my family too. My daddy stayed, and I have no idea how he did or why, but I thank God every day for His will and plan. I await the next dance with my daddy. I'm Cinderella, my shoe fits, and I'm right where I'm meant to be. I am in the arms of Jesus. I'm a daddy's girl again, but this time to a heavenly Father.

———

*God, you are filled with so much wonder. I give
you all of the glory, Lord. God, your word is a
healing song. Heal your brokenhearted girls, your*

Cinderellas who got lost along the way. Heal the ones who were abandoned by their dad. Show them, Lord, that there is hope in You for healing through this heartbreak. Heavenly Father, only You satisfy. For those running away from facing their past trauma, God, show them that running will only take away more time from living in freedom and redemption. Thank you that we are Yours, God. Thank you for setting your sons and daughters free every day.

God, I pray that everyone who reads this will be touched, transformed, healed, delivered, redeemed, restored, saved, and born again by God Himself. Thank you for the cross, thank you for repentance, obedience, and salvation. I never knew I could be loved like this. Thank you, God, for answering my prayers. Thank you, God, for changing my life.

—⧛—

In Luke 9:23–24, Jesus "said to the crowd if any of you wants to be my follower, you must give up your own way, take up your cross daily, and follow me. If you try to hang on to your life you will lose it. But if you give up your life for my sake, you will save it." Now we are those who follow Jesus. The moment I chose God, I was seated with Christ. "For he raised us from the dead along with Christ and seated us with Him in the heavenly realms because we are united with Christ Jesus." Jesus is right here with us, and the Holy Spirit is within us.

—⧛—

God thank you for the people who will read this and choose you today. Thank you for the beginning of our love story and the start of Your love story with others. God bless your children reading this, so they will open their hearts and surrender their lives to You, now and forever. God, thank you for writing this book for the once lost that You have now found. Amen!